Internal Administrative Organization In Teachers Colleges

By

ROBERT H. MORRISON, Ph.D.

Teachers College, Columbia University
Contributions to Education,
No. 592

Published with the Approval of
Professor EDWARD S. EVENDEN,
Sponsor

BUREAU OF PUBLICATIONS
Teachers College, Columbia University
NEW YORK CITY

1933

PRINTED IN THE UNITED STATES OF AMERICA
AT THE COUNTRY LIFE PRESS
GARDEN CITY, NEW YORK

ACKNOWLEDGMENTS

The author desires to acknowledge his grateful appreciation to Professor E. S. Evenden, whose guidance and counsel in the development of this study were invaluable. To Professor William C. Bagley the author owes much for the inspiring and helpful suggestions made during the progress of the study. To Professor John K. Norton he is indebted for constructive criticism in assembling and interpreting the data.

The author is especially indebted to the one hundred fifty teachers college presidents who furnished data, to the members of the jury of teachers college presidents who evaluated the criteria which deal with internal administrative organization, and to Harry A. Sprague, President of the New Jersey State Teachers College at Montclair, and to George W. Frasier, President of the Colorado State Teachers College at Greeley, for their encouragement and sympathetic cooperation.

Finally, the author acknowledges that without the constant and untiring assistance of Mabel Hebeler Morrison the study could not have been accomplished.

R. H. M.

CONTENTS

Contents

Contents

TABLES

FIGURES

Internal
Administrative Organization
In Teachers Colleges

CHAPTER I

THE DEVELOPMENT OF THE PROBLEM

I. INTRODUCTION

FOR nearly a century the American people have been developing state-supported institutions for the training of teachers. The beginning of these institutions was in 1839. During that year Massachusetts established two normal schools: one at Barre and the other at Lexington. Since that time other states have continued to establish similar institutions. At the present time there are state normal schools or teachers colleges in all but four states in the Union. These states are Florida, Utah, Wyoming, and South Carolina. The Office of Education in its 1931 directory reports 225 as the number of state- or city-controlled institutions for the professional education of teachers. This report does not include schools of education in state universities. It is evident from these facts that the various states in the nation believe in the education of teachers in institutions specifically charged with that responsibility.

The enrollment[1] in the first institutions was limited to a small group. The school at Barre opened with three students and closed the first year with twelve. Bridgewater Normal School enrolled a total of 59 students in its tenth year of service. West Newton reports 102 as its greatest number during its tenth year. At that time all administrative functions were on the personal basis and little or no internal administrative organization is reported in the historical accounts of these early normal schools. However, as the number of students entering those institutions increased, it became desirable to develop an administrative staff whose duty it is to perform those service functions which will make the teaching program more effective and of greater value to the students.

There were no professional books on education to guide the chief executives in their development of the early normal

[1]Barnard, Henry, *Normal Schools and Other Institutions, Agencies, and Means Designed for the Professional Education of Teachers*, Vol. I.

1

schools.   Until recently each normal school or teachers college
has been dependent almost solely upon the educational foresight
and ability of its president and staff to develop its program.
The literature dealing with the problems of the professional
education of teachers has developed largely during the past
twenty-five years. Hall-Quest,[2] in writing about the science of
education, points out that as late as 1898 education as a pro-
fession was not recognized.   Since that time research studies
in considerable numbers have thrown light upon various phases
of education.   School administration and organization have
naturally been subjects for research.   The Missouri survey by
the Carnegie Foundation, begun in 1915 and the findings published in 1920 under the leadership of Dr. William S. Learned
and Dr. William C. Bagley, is a far-reaching scientific study
which has contributed greatly to shaping educational policies
in professional schools for teachers.   It has stimulated much
additional research and writing in the field of professional education of teachers.   To-day the president of a normal school or
teachers college can find some educational writings which deal
with almost every problem in his field.

II. THE GENERAL PROBLEM OF THE STUDY

In the present situation there are more than two hundred
state institutions which have been established for the professional education of teachers.   Nearly all of these have an
internal administrative organization which has developed from
the personal to a largely impersonal basis.

What are the criteria which control the internal administrative organizations within these institutions?   Which of these
criteria are considered valid by leaders in the field of teachers
college administration?   How do practices concerning administrative organization measure up to criteria validated by
leaders in the field?   Can an internal administrative organization be suggested which is practical and yet conforms to
standards set up in validated criteria?

III. THE NEED FOR THE STUDY

Although there is some educational literature dealing with
internal administrative organization in teachers colleges, for

[2]Hall-Quest, Alfred Lawrence, *Professional Secondary Education in Teachers Colleges*, pp. 1–3.

the most part it is scattered and not organized around the topic. There is no organized statement of criteria which specifically concern this topic of internal administrative organization. There are several such criteria stated separately and each is approved by a leader in the field. These need to be brought together and submitted to a group of experts for validation. An integrated picture of internal organization is needed in order that any president of a teachers college may compare the administrative practices in the institution over which he presides with practices found in institutions of comparable size. Data for such comparisons are now lacking.

Descriptions of specific features of administrative organization are either lacking entirely or presented in limited detail. The kinds and scope of committees organized and the procedures used in controlling and guiding them need to be tabulated and presented for a large enough number of teachers colleges to assure a fairly accurate and complete picture. A summary of the interrelationships of administrative officers will provide suggestive data for presidents who are seeking to improve such relationships within their particular institutions. Finally, the sharing by administrative officers and other staff members in the formulation of policies and the performance of functions needs to be shown in order to make possible, in the light of validated criteria, a critical analysis of the present situation regarding administrative organization.

IV. PURPOSES OF THE STUDY

The purposes of this study, then, are to meet the needs stated above and to suggest an internal administrative organization which will conform to principles of educational administration and at the same time incorporate the better practices found in different institutions which are now in successful operation.

The following specific questions will be discussed:

1. What are the various criteria for evaluating internal administrative organization in teachers colleges as advocated by:

A. Writers in the field of teachers college administration?

B. Presidents who are administering teachers colleges?

2. What agreement is there among a group of superior administrators of teachers colleges concerning the desirability

of the administrative conditions represented by these criteria?

3. How do presidents organize and use committees in the administration of teachers colleges?

4. What are the interrelations of administrative officers within teachers colleges?

5. What are the various administrative functions and to whom are they delegated for control and performance?

V. THE SCOPE OF THE STUDY

This investigation is limited to internal administrative organization as found in 150 teachers colleges in 41 states. A majority of all the state and municipal teachers colleges established within each of these 41 states is included in this study. Table I shows that the sampling of institutions is well distributed throughout the various geographical regions of the nation. The classification of institutions by enrollment shows that the investigation includes 22 colleges enrolling fewer than 300 students, 68 colleges enrolling 300 to 799 students, 27 colleges enrolling 800 to 1199 students, and 33 colleges enrolling 1200 or more students. It is believed that the data are representative of the internal administrative situation as it exists.

VI. PROCEDURES

Criteria for evaluating internal administrative organization in teachers colleges were formulated from three sources: (*a*) the literature dealing with college administration, (*b*) statements in college catalogs, (*c*) interviews with administrators and staff members from teachers colleges. These criteria were refined through seminar conferences and then submitted to a jury of thirty teachers college presidents for validation.[3] The presidents requested to serve on this jury were selected as follows:

1. Each president contributing data for the investigation was requested to submit the names of six other presidents whom he considered superior administrators.

2. From this list of presidents designated as superior and

---

[3] A statement of the criteria as submitted to the jury appears in Appendix A.

TABLE I

STATES FROM WHICH ONE OR MORE TEACHERS COLLEGES OR NORMAL SCHOOLS
COOPERATED IN A STUDY OF INTERNAL ADMINISTRATIVE ORGANIZATION.
1932

State	Number of Colleges Cooperating	State	Number of Colleges Cooperating
Alabama	3	Montana	2
Arizona	2	Nebraska	4
Arkansas	2	New Hampshire	1
California	6	New Jersey	5
Colorado	2	New Mexico	2
Connecticut	4	North Carolina	3
Georgia	1	North Dakota	3
Idaho	1	New York*	12
Illinois*	7	Ohio	3
Indiana*	3	Oklahoma	4
Iowa	1	Oregon	3
Kansas	3	Pennsylvania	10
Kentucky	2	Rhode Island	1
Louisiana	1	South Dakota	3
Maine	2	Tennessee	4
Maryland	3	Texas	7
Massachusetts	6	Virginia	4
Michigan	4	Washington	3
Minnesota	5	West Virginia	3
Mississippi	2	Wisconsin	6
Missouri*	7		

Total number of colleges cooperating 150

*Municipal teachers colleges from Illinois, Indiana, Missouri, and New York contributed data for this study.

actively engaged in teachers college administration thirty who met the following standards were chosen:

A. Designation as superior by at least three presidents, each located in a different geographical region of the United States.
B. Designation as superior by a president from the same state. In cases like Iowa, where there is but one teachers college, designation as superior by a president in an adjoining state satisfied this standard.
C. Special study and achievement in education as evidenced by the holding of an advanced degree or authorship of a book in education.

It is believed that these standards assured the selection of a jury whose members are held in high repute by their colleagues within the same state and whose achievements are such that they are known nationally.

A questionnaire was designed to secure data concerning internal administrative organization and was sent to the presidents of all state and municipal teachers colleges listed in the *1931 Educational Directory* of the United States Office of Education. The tabulation and interpretation of these data in the light of the criteria as stated and validated appear in the following chapters.

VII. RELIABILITY OF THE DATA

The questionnaire used in collecting the data was sponsored by the National Survey of the Education of Teachers, and it was sent out by the United States Office of Education. It was also approved by the Committee on Standards and Surveys of the American Association of Teachers Colleges. The chairman of that committee, Dr. H. L. Donovan, President of the State Teachers College at Richmond, Kentucky, wrote a letter to presidents of the teachers colleges in the Association, requesting cooperation in furnishing data for the investigation. It is believed that sponsorship of these two organizations contributed toward a high degree of completeness in the reported data.

Two other means were used to insure accuracy. Items in the questionnaire were, wherever possible, checked against statements in the catalog of the institution concerned. If data reported in the questionnaire differed from data given in the catalog, a letter of inquiry was sent to the president, asking which data were correct. Another means used to check accuracy was the construction of the questionnaire in such a way as to have some items check others. An illustration will make this matter clear. Concerning each official this question was asked: "What other college offices, if any, does this official hold?" If the director of placement was listed as holding the office of director of training, then it would follow that the director of training would be listed as holding the office of director of placement. Each report was studied carefully for inconsistencies. In a few cases inconsistent data were discovered too late to permit checking.   Such data are not included in the tabulations.

VIII. ORGANIZATION OF THE STUDY

Chapter I states the problem, introduces the study, and describes the procedures used.   Chapter II presents a statement of criteria validated by the judgment of 30 teachers college presidents.   These presidents were rated as superior administrators by the 150 teachers college presidents who furnished data for the study.   In Chapter III committees are discussed. This discussion shows the present status of committees organized in teachers colleges, conflicting viewpoints concerning the use of committees, and the procedures followed by presidents in controlling committees.   Chapter IV contains a discussion of the interrelations of the chief administrative officers in teachers colleges.   The performance of administrative functions which results from the delegation of authority is tabulated and discussed in Chapter V.   A general summary and recommendations appear in Chapter VI.

CHAPTER II

CRITERIA FOR EVALUATING INTERNAL ADMINIS-
TRATIVE ORGANIZATION IN TEACHERS COLLEGES

ADMINISTRATIVE organization in teachers colleges should be planned to render services to the students and to the teaching personnel. The amount of service needed will depend upon the size of the student body and the variety of activities which the institution deems essential in the education of teachers for its constituency. Diversity in administrative organization is to be expected and in many cases is undoubtedly desirable. This diversity may be due to differences in individual administrators, to differences in the personnel with whom the administrators work, or to the practice of solving administrative problems according to some temporary expedient.

The purpose of this chapter is to state and evaluate some criteria which may be utilized in appraising practices found in administrative organizations. Careful study of the literature which deals with college administration reveals a number of criteria approved by different students in the field. These criteria, as explained in Chapter I, were formulated and submitted for rating to a jury of thirty administrators named as superior by teachers college presidents.[1]

The validation of proposed policies through group judgment is an established procedure. Taylor,[2] in discussing criteria for school supply management, contends that public opinion gives credence to expert judgment not only in the fields of law, medicine, engineering, and government, but also in the field of education.

Evaluation by jury rating has been used in educational research by several investigators. A jury selected because of special ability in the particular field concerned is often used to judge validity of principles and practices. Charters and

---

[1]See Appendix A for a statement of the criteria as submitted to the jury.
[2]Taylor, Robert B., *Principles of School Supply Management*, p. 12.

8

Waples,[3] after making an exhaustive analysis of the duties of teachers, used a jury to validate the relative importance and difficulty of the various activities involved.   Rutledge[4] stated ninety-six principles for the administration of teachers colleges and normal schools and submitted these principles for validation to a jury of outstanding men in the field of educational administration.

The selection of the jury which rated the criteria in this chapter was made by presidents of teachers colleges from among their own number.   The standards for the selection of the jurors, as previously stated in Chapter I, page 5, restricted membership in the jury to those presidents each of whom has a reputation national in scope and whose achievement is such that a president in a near-by teachers college designated him as a superior administrator.   It is believed that the judgment of such a jury is more trustworthy than any other evaluation not based upon data secured by controlled experimentation. The administrative experience of the jurors varies in length from two to forty-four years.   The quartile points in the range of experience are as follows: Q_1 equals 6, Q_2 equals 11, Q_3 equals 19.   Presidents with experience as indicated by these data have had contacts with administrative organization during a sufficient length of time to give weight to their evaluations.

More than half the members of the jury, selected to evaluate the criteria in this chapter, have advanced degrees from Columbia, Harvard, Iowa, New York, Peabody, and other colleges of education.   It seems reasonable to assume that the members of the jury have adapted to their particular institutions the principles of educational administration as taught in our leading universities.

Presidents of teachers colleges, through contacts with department heads and members of the professorial staff within their institutions, have been compelled to consider departmental viewpoints in the formulation of institutional policies.   This consideration of such viewpoints by presidents adds to their desirable qualifications to serve on a jury which validates criteria for administrative organization.   Successful administra-

---

[3]Charters, W. W. and Waples, Douglas, *The Commonwealth Teacher Training Study*, Summary Table A, pp. 493–535.
[4]Rutledge, Samuel A., *The Development of Guiding Principles for the Administration of Teachers Colleges and Normal Schools*, Chap. II and III.

tion requires special study. Presidents have been forced to make this study. In addition, the very nature of their work gives them a theoretical and empirical background. Because of these considerations a jury of teachers college presidents selected in accordance with standards previously enumerated should bring to the task of validating criteria the value of experience, the influence of the science of educational administration, the results of educational research, and the integrated institutional viewpoint which comes from a consideration of the problems of many individual staff members and departmental groups.

For the purposes of this study it is believed that a jury of thirty is sufficiently reliable. Charters and Waples[5] found that the predicted coefficient of correlation between the judgment scores of one group of twenty-five persons and an infinite number was .949± .015. This correlation indicates that the judgment scores of thirty jurors as used in this study would be changed but little by increasing the size of the jury.

In order to learn which criteria, if any, depend upon reasonably adequate financial support for validity, each juror was requested to rate each criterion twice. In the first rating reasonably adequate financial support was assumed. In the second rating curtailed or limited financial support was assumed. Each juror designated each criterion by one of the following five characteristics: (*a*) highly desirable, (*b*) desirable, (*c*) of no particular value but not undesirable, (*d*) undesirable, or (*e*) harmful. A summary of these designations with an index rating[6] for each criterion appears in Table II.

Criterion 1.

Administrative organization should provide for the performance of essentially the same administrative functions in all teachers colleges.[7]

This criterion emphasizes that teachers colleges are alike in functions to be performed. The administrative organization must provide for a number of closely interrelated functions, all

---

[5]Charters, W. W. and Waples, Douglas, *The Commonwealth Teacher-Training Study*, p. 70.
[6]See Appendix B for an explanation of the procedure used in arriving at values for index ratings.
[7]Brunstetter, M. R., *Business Management in School Systems of Different Sizes*, p. 8.   Leonard, R. J., Evenden, E. S., and O'Rear, F. B., *Survey of Higher Education for the United Lutheran Church in America*, Vol. II, p. 3.

TABLE II

AN EVALUATION RATING BY THIRTY SUPERIOR ADMINISTRATORS OF TWENTY
CRITERIA FOR INTERNAL ADMINISTRATIVE ORGANIZATION IN TEACHERS COLLEGES[1]

Statement of Criteria	Financial Support Reasonably Adequate						Financial Support Curtailed or Limited					
	Highly Desirable 1.0	Desirable 0.5	Of No Particular Value But Not Undesirable 0.0	Undesirable −0.5	Harmful −1.0	Index Rating [2]	Highly Desirable 1.0	Desirable 0.5	Of No Particular Value But Not Undesirable 0.0	Undesirable −0.5	Harmful −1.0	Index Rating [2]
1. Administrative organization should provide for the performance of essentially the same administrative functions in all teachers colleges. An administrative function in this criterion refers to such activities as classification of students, preparing the budget, etc...	14[3]	13	2	1	0	+.66	16	12	2	0	0	+.73
2. As the enrollment becomes greater, administrative organization should provide for greater specialization of duties of the various officials...................	17	10	3	0	0	+.73	14	14	2	0	0	+.70
3. Administrative organization should provide opportunity for the instructional staff to teach in their various departments without being overburdened with administrative duties.............	28	2	0	0	0	+.97	23	7	0	0	0	+.91
4. Administrative organization should provide, in so far as possible, for freeing the president from the performance of a multiplicity of duties which may occupy his time to such an extent that major attention cannot be given to the development of administrative and institutional policies.............	27	3	0	0	0	+.95	16	9	2	2	1	+.61
5. Administrative organization should provide for the utilization of an administrative council, chosen by the president to serve him in an advisory capacity concerning formation of policies and the making of administrative decisions on which the faculty as a whole is not informed. This criterion does not mean that final decisions should be made by the council rather than the president	18	6	0	0	1	+.05	15	9	2	2	1	+.58

TABLE II—(*Continued*)

Statement of Criteria	Financial Support Reasonably Adequate						Financial Support Curtailed or Limited					
	Highly Desirable 1.0	Desirable 0.5	Of No Particular Value But Not Undesirable 0.0	Undesirable −0.5	Harmful −1.0	Index Rating	Highly Desirable 1.0	Desirable 0.5	Of No Particular Value But Not Undesirable 0.0	Undesirable −0.5	Harmful −1.0	Index Rating
6. If an administrative council is used, the internal organization of the college should provide for faculty representation on the council......	17	7	3	2	1	+.61	17	7	3	2	1	+.61
7. If an administrative council is used, it should consist of heads of departments....	6	6	10	8	0	+.17	6	5	12	5	2	+.13
8. Administrative organization should provide special committees for investigations requiring special study	20	9	0	1	0	+.80	17	12	0	1	0	+.75
9. Administrative organization should provide for the selection of standing and special committees by the president..................	19	7	2	0	2	+.68	19	7	2	1	1	+.70
10. Administrative organization should provide for the selection of standing and special committees by the faculty or representatives of the faculty.................	2	3	5	15	5	−.30	2	3	5	15	5	−.30
11. Administrative organization should provide few, if any, standing committees for the administration of functions.................	12	6	0	11	1	+.28	10	5	1	13	1	+.17
12. Administrative organization should provide standing committees for the administration of all major groups of functions...............	5	5	3	8	9	−.18	5	5	4	7	9	−.17
13. Administrative organization should provide a fixed procedure for replacing membership in standing committees...................	6	12	5	5	2	+.25	7	13	5	4	1	+.35
14. When standing committees are used, administrative organization should provide for keeping membership and chairmanship constant in so far as possible........	2	21	1	3	3	+.27	1	22	2	2	3	+.27

TABLE II—(*Continued*)

Statement of Criteria	Financial Support Reasonably Adequate						Financial Support Curtailed or Limited					
	Highly Desirable 1.0	Desirable 0.5	Of No Particular Value But Not Undesirable 0.0	Undesirable −0.5	Harmful −1.0	Index Rating	Highly Desirable 1.0	Desirable 0.5	Of No Particular Value But Not Undesirable 0.0	Undesirable −0.5	Harmful −1.0	Index Rating
15. Administrative organization should provide for the participation of the whole faculty in suggesting or formulating policies concerning instruction............	17	6	4	3	0	+.62	17	6	6	1	0	+.65
16. Administrative organization should provide for faculty approval of all major administrative policies.....	7	9	1	8	5	+.08	5	11	1	8	5	+.05
17. Administrative organization should provide for the grouping of related functions under the direction or control of an officer who in turn is responsible to the president......................	21	3	2	3	1	+.67	18	6	3	3	0	+.65
18. Administrative organization should provide for the centering of responsibility in individuals rather than in groups..................	18	7	0	5	0	+.65	16	8	1	5	0	+.58
19. Administrative organization should provide for the approval of policies by the state board of control......	12	11	3	1	3	+.47	12	12	2	1	3	+.48
20. Administrative organization should provide for the making of final decisions by the president after policies have been approved by the state board of control. This criterion is not to be interpreted as interfering with the president's delegating to a subordinate officer authority to make decisions..........	18	10	0	1	1	+.71	19	9	0	1	1	+.73

[1]Two ratings are given to show which criteria, if any, depend upon reasonably adequate financial support for validity.

[2]Index values; see Appendix B. The index rating should be interpreted as follows: +.6 to +1.0 highly desirable, +.2 to +.59 desirable, 0.0 to +.19 probably desirable, 0.0 to −.19 probably undesirable, −.2 to −.59 undesirable, −.6 to −1.0 harmful.

[3]This table should be read as follows: With financial support reasonably adequate, 14 judges rated Criterion 1 as 1.0 or highly desirable, 13 judges rated it 0.5 or desirable, etc.

of which must receive careful planning if the institution is to succeed. For example, admission of students, housing, providing a curriculum, classroom instruction, supply management, health service, social activities, library service, budgetary planning, accounting, and many others are functions for which the internal administrative organization in every teachers college must provide. The size of the student body, the length or the variety of the curricula offered, may cause variations in the emphasis accorded certain aspects of administration, but every important function must be provided for. Table II shows that the jury recognized this principle as highly desirable. One juror rated this principle as undesirable for those institutions which have reasonably adequate financial support. He commented: "With financial support reasonably adequate, teachers colleges might reasonably develop a few features of experimentation not adapted to other institutions."

Criterion 2.

As the enrollment becomes greater, administrative organization should provide for greater specialization of the duties of various officials.[8]

The number of individuals necessary for administrative service and the amount of time required will depend upon the size of the institution. In a small teachers college, an executive may perform several functions, or particular aspects of the work may be delegated to persons who devote part time to class instruction and part time to administrative duties. In large teachers colleges there is usually a sufficient amount of work to require the services of one or more specially trained administrative assistants. For example, in a small institution the director of personnel may serve as registrar, dean of women, director of housing, and director of placement of teachers. In a large institution the director of personnel may supervise all of these functional services, but there is likely to be an administrative assistant in charge of each. The high index rating shown in Table II indicates that the jury of administrators rates this criterion as highly desirable both when finances are reasonably adequate and when financial support is limited or curtailed.

[8]Reeder, W. G., *The Business Administration of a School System*, p. 37. Leonard, R. J., Evenden, E. S., O'Rear, F. B., *Survey of Higher Education for the United Lutheran Church in America*, Vol. II, p. 4.

Criterion 3.

Administrative organization should provide opportunity for the instructional staff to teach in their various departments without being overburdened with administrative duties.[9]

Energy used in administration cannot be used in preparation for teaching, in actual classroom instruction, or in extra-curricular activities. Administration, though important, is secondary to teaching either in the classroom or through extra-curricular activities. Those administrative officers whose teaching load is heavy are probably unable to render efficient service either in the classroom or in administration. During periods of unusual strain which practically every administrative organization faces at times, classroom instruction is likely to be slighted because of the pressure of administrative duties. Keeping up in both instruction and administration divides the interest and increases the load.

Since the sole objective of a teachers college is to provide professional education for its students, it would seem unwise to hamper both administration and teaching by assigning heavy teaching loads to administrative officers or heavy administrative duties to the teaching staff.

Table II shows that the jury rates this criterion as representing a very desirable administrative condition.

The index rating is higher when financial support is reasonably adequate. The index rating is lower when finances are limited or curtailed. One juror commented: "Even with finances curtailed the teaching by the staff must not be hampered."

Criterion 4.

Administrative organization must provide, in so far as possible, for freeing the president from the performance of a mulitplicity of duties which may occupy his time to such an extent that major attention cannot be given to the development of administrative and institutional policies.[10]

The president must have a vision of the functioning of the whole institution. He needs to integrate and coordinate all

[9]Agnew, W. D., *The Administration of Professional Schools for Teachers*, p. 202. Klein, Arthur J., *Survey of Land Grant Colleges and Universities*, Vol. I, p. 75.
[10]Moehlman, Arthur B., *A Survey of the Needs of the Michigan State Normal Schools*, p. 143. Judd, Charles H. and Others, *Report of a Survey of the State Institutions of Higher Learning in Indiana*, p. 92.

phases of the college in order that each may make its maximum contribution. All other officers will probably have special viewpoints. The president needs to balance and use each of these viewpoints in developing a program for the professional education of teachers. If the president, either voluntarily or through compulsion, gives too much attention to details which yield him little or no understanding of the problems of the institution and which might be attended to by other members of the administrative staff, he consumes time and energy which could be devoted to bigger problems.

Conditions change, and as they change, policies must often be modified or replaced in order to meet the new conditions. Unless the president has time to study the situation as a whole, he will probably be unable to integrate the various phases of the institution or to maintain sound and adequate policies. Table II, page 11, shows that freedom from a multiplicity of duties is considered a very desirable administrative condition by the jurors who rated the criteria. When financial support is limited or curtailed, the jury gives a much lower index rating. This indicates that a president with limited support is forced to do things somewhat differently.

Criterion 5.

Administrative organization should provide for the utilization of an administrative council, chosen by the president to serve him in an advisory capacity concerning formation of policies and the making of administrative decisions on which the faculty as a whole is not informed.[11]

The president may need such a council to balance any peculiar ways he may have of viewing problems, and to help him overcome any possible bias or prejudice. Group judgment is a necessary safeguard against individualism and bias. An institution under the complete jurisdiction of a president, regardless of his ability, may become highly individualistic. In the consideration of instructional problems faculty deliberations and judgments are highly desirable. The writer believes that the discussion of administrative problems by a group such as is here proposed is equally desirable.

[11]Survey of Education in Utah, pp. 286–287. Capen, Samuel P. and Stevens, Edwin B., *Survey of the University of Nevada*, p. 86. Lindsay, E. E. and Holland E. O., *College and University Administration*, p. 466. Rutledge, S. A., *The Development of Guiding Principles for the Administration of Teachers Colleges and Normal Schools*, p. 23.

The administrative council gives the president a means of forecasting reactions to proposed administrative measures. It is assumed the membership of the administrative council will be selected in such a way that some member on the council will be well informed concerning each of the major administrative divisions of public relations, finance, instruction, personnel and faculty personnel relationships. The council, if encouraged to do so, can point out how any proposed measure will affect the various phases of the institution's work. The council may offer suggestions which will refine and strengthen the proposed measure or it may offer objections which will lead the president to withdraw the proposal. To be of greatest service to the president, the council must subject each proposal to its greatest possible criticism and suggest other possible alternatives, always leaving the president free to make the final decision.

Table II shows that the jurors rated this criterion as highly desirable when financial support is reasonably adequate. A few jurors rated the criterion less desirable when finances are curtailed. The comment of one president is especially pertinent at this point. He wrote: "An administrative council often fails to see the need for economy. The council members are likely to urge the development of a program which cannot be financed. In such circumstances the president is better off without a council."

Criterion 6.

If an administrative council is used, the internal organization of the college should provide for faculty representation on the council.[12]

Such representation is advocated by some as a means of giving the faculty a voice in administration. It is contended that this procedure contributes to faculty morale and assures those members of the staff who devote full time to instruction that their problems will receive attention by the administration. A different viewpoint was expressed by one juror who rated the criterion as harmful. He commented: "A representative of the faculty may render splendid service on the administrative council or he may assume that all administrators are in league

[12]Foster, William T., "Faculty Participation in College Government," *School and Society,* pp. 594–596, April 22, 1916. Lindsay, E. E. and Holland, E. O., *College and University Administration,* pp. 461–472.

against the instructional staff.   Such an assumption may cause him to propose plans and policies which the president may consider dangerous or unwise at the time.   If his plans are not adopted, he may consider it necessary to report to his constituency.   Such a report can lead to no good.   After such a report the president hardly dares remove him from the council.   The problem is much easier if each member of the council conceives his task as an adviser of the president and not as a representative of any group."

Table II shows that the jury rated this criterion equally high with Criterion 5.   The two do not conflict.   Either criterion could, according to the jury, represent desirable practice.

Criterion 7.
If an administrative council is used, it should consist of heads of departments.

The index rating in Table II, page 11, shows that the jury rated this criterion as representative of an administrative condition which is probably desirable.   However, the index rating is so low that it is probably unsafe to follow it as a guide in administrative procedures.

One juror objected to a council made up of department heads only, because the staff members who could be of greatest assistance might not be included.   On the other hand, there may be department heads not particularly adapted to serve on an administrative council.   Efficient administration would not require them to devote time and energy to council service.

Criterion 8.
Administrative organization should provide special committees for investigations requiring special study.[13]

This criterion, if practiced, makes all of the expertness on the staff available to the administration in investigating and securing facts necessary in reaching a decision.   If members of the committee happen to be vitally concerned in the problem which caused the investigation, they will be in a better position to help solve the problem because they helped in the investigation.   Such committee service may prove to be an excellent

[13]Rutledge, S. A., *The Development of Guiding Principles for the Administration of Teachers Colleges and Normal Schools*, p. 24.   Klein, Arthur J., *Survey of Land Grant Colleges and Universities*, Vol. I, p. 75.

means to train faculty members while in service and at the same time acquaint the faculty with administrative problems.

Table II shows high agreement concerning the desirability of special committees for investigations.

Criterion 9.

Administrative organization should provide for the selection of standing and special committees by the president.[14]

Table II shows that this criterion is rated by a large percentage of the jurors as highly desirable. One juror rated it undesirable. He commented: "Committees selected by the faculty will consider their selection a vote of confidence by their colleagues. If appointed by the president, the committee assignment will be just another task." Committee work is not a mark of honor or distinction. A task needs to be done. The president is responsible. By appointing the committee he can select those capable of rendering the best service and make them responsible to him for results.

Criterion 10.

Administrative organization should provide for the selection of standing and special committees by the faculty or representatives of the faculty.

Table II shows a small percentage of the presidents favoring this criterion. A much larger percentage of the jurors rates it undesirable or harmful. The index rating is negative and low enough to warrant the rejection of the criterion as invalid. Since it is directly opposed to Criterion 9, all statements supporting that criterion are in opposition to this one.

Criterion 11.

Administrative organization should provide few, if any, standing committees for the administration of functions.[15]

The worth of faculty committees for administrative purposes is seriously questioned. The duties are usually assigned in addition to an otherwise full program. Valuable time of faculty members may easily be wasted in heavy committee assignments.

[14]Sherrod, C. C., *The Administration of State Teachers Colleges through Faculty Committees,* p. 73.   Foster, William T., "Faculty Participation in College Administration," *School and Society,* April 22, 1916, pp. 594–595.   Rutledge, S. A., *The Development of Guiding Principles for the Administration of Teachers Colleges and Normal Schools,* pp. 23–24.

[15]Rutledge, S. A., *The Development of Guiding Principles for the Administration of Teachers Colleges and Normal Schools,* p. 24.

Some authorities[16] believe that administrative work attempted by committees would be better performed if given to responsible individuals. Individuals are more likely to specialize their knowledge and less likely to vacillate in their decisions. When administrative functions are performed by individuals, the responsibility for decisions is more quickly located.

Table II shows a clear-cut difference of opinion on the part of the members of the jury validating the criteria. The majority of presidents on the jury favor few committees for administrative purposes. On the other hand, twelve jurors think that limitation of committees is undesirable. Some jurors judged the criterion as of less value in institutions wherein financial support is curtailed or limited. Table II, page 11, shows that the members of the jury are either definitely in favor of or definitely opposed to this criterion. Not one of the jurors designated it as representing an administrative condition of "no particular value but not undesirable." The index rating is low because positive and negative ratings tend to balance each other.

Criterion 12.

Administrative organization should provide standing committees for the administration of all major groups of functions.[17]

This criterion is directly opposed to the previous one. Its index rating is negative. Although it has some proponents on the jury who rate it as highly desirable, there is a larger number who consider it harmful. The chief arguments advanced against the use of committees for administration are the difficulty involved in fixing responsibility, and the loss of time which is necessarily involved in committee assignments.

Criterion 13.

Administrative organization should provide a fixed procedure for replacing membership in standing committees.[18]

Many administrators believe that some standing committees are desirable. A standing committee can work continuously on the formulation of policies for presentation to the faculty. Such continuous work prevents snap judgment and provides

[16]Reeves, Floyd W. and Russell, John Dale, *College Organization and Administration*, p. 75.
[17]Sherrod, C. C., *The Administration of State Teachers Colleges through Faculty Committees*, p. 73.
[18]Rutledge, S. A., *The Development of Guiding Principles for the Administration of Teachers Colleges and Normal Schools*, p. 24.

an organization which makes previous committee efforts more readily understood for subsequent investigations. A standing committee is already organized for considering problems which arise unexpectedly. This gives an administrator a means for handling certain investigations or for securing group judgment on certain problems without creating a special committee for the purpose. However, standing committees are likely to assume an executive function unless there is a fixed procedure for changing membership. This fixed procedure can well be a definite limitation upon the time which a member may serve. As soon as a standing committee assumes that it has sole prerogative in the function for which it was organized, it may resent encroachment by executive officers or by the faculty as a whole. When this happens, it becomes administrative rather than legislative and in a large measure loses its usefulness.

Table II shows a low but positive index rating for the desirability of this criterion.

Criterion 14.

When standing committees are used, administrative organization should provide for keeping membership and chairmanship constant in so far as possible.

This criterion is in conflict with Criterion 13. Those jurors who rated this criterion as highly desirable rated Criterion 13 as harmful. This rating emphasizes conflicting viewpoints concerning the use of committees in administration. One juror commented: "When standing committees are used for the administration of functions they become efficient through service. Frequent changes decrease efficiency. There should be a regular way to change committee members if such a plan does not operate to force efficient members from committee service."

Criterion 15.

Administrative organization should provide for the participation of the whole faculty in suggesting or formulating policies concerning instruction.[19]

Within each teachers college faculty are individuals whose experience and training are such that their judgments are of

[19]Foster, William T., "Faculty Participation in College Government," *School and Society*, April 22, 1918, pp. 594–597. McVey, F. L., "Administrative Relations in College," *School and Society*, December 8, 1928, pp. 705–709. *Missouri Survey of Higher Education*, p. 386.

distinct value in determining administrative policies. Efficiency demands that these abilities should be used. The efficient administrator will seek faculty judgment not for the sake of democracy but for the sake of efficiency. It seems reasonable to assume that faculty judgment, when based upon the opinions of large majorities, and upon matters in which all members are informed, is much safer than individual judgment. Also, when the members of a faculty are evenly divided over an issue, it would seem unwise to introduce a new policy. The importance of maintaining that intangible condition known as good faculty morale cannot be overestimated. Morale is much more likely to be high if a faculty is carrying forward policies which the large majority of its members thoroughly understands and approves.

Table II, page 11, shows that a majority of the jurors rates this criterion as highly desirable, both when finances are reasonably adequate and when they are curtailed.

Criterion 16.

Administrative organization should provide for faculty approval of all major administrative policies.[20]

Table II, page 11, shows a low but positive index rating for this criterion. An analysis of the ratings indicates that the jury of selected presidents is quite evenly divided. Approximately half of the jury believes that provision for faculty approval of administrative policies is desirable, while an equal number rates it undesirable or harmful. Those jurors favoring the criterion contend that such a policy assures faculty cooperation and promotes a spirit of democracy in the institution. Those of the jury who oppose the criterion contend that the faculty as a whole is not informed concerning administrative policies other than those related to instruction. One president commented: "Nearly all faculty members concentrate their study and thinking on the instructional problems of one department. Few of them are interested or informed concerning institutional administrative problems. They lack information and viewpoint necessary for approving or denying administrative policies."

---

[20]Foster, William T., "Faculty Participation in College Government," *School and Society*, April 22, 1916, p. 597.

Criterion 17.

Administrative organization should provide for the grouping of related functions under the direction or control of an officer who in turn is responsible to the president.[21]

It seems reasonable to assume that the grouping of related functions will tend to increase efficiency. Related functions support each other. The training required for the preparation of the business officer is quite different from that required as preparation for registrar or librarian. On the other hand, the registrar is bound to become well acquainted with the abilities of the students by the time they are ready to apply for positions. This knowledge would be of great assistance in the placement of graduates, but of little or no value in carrying forward the business management of the institution. Then, too, related functions grouped under the control of one officer should prevent a duplication of effort. If the related functions are too numerous for one official to perform, assistants working under his direction can be appointed. This grouping of related functions with assistants responsible to one director should unify and integrate the administrative program and, at the same time, increase efficiency.

Table II, page 11, shows that a majority of the selected jury of presidents rates this criterion as highly desirable.

Criterion 18.

Administrative organization should provide for the centering of responsibility for the performance of duties in individuals rather than in groups.[22]

Whenever administrative responsibility is delegated to a group rather than an individual, the total number of people carrying responsibility is increased. The carrying of needless responsibility wastes the teaching energies of the institution. If a group rather than an individual has responsibility, the chief executive cannot give credit to an individual for tasks well performed or censure any one individual for duties neglected. When groups perform functions there is likely to be confusion resulting from duplication of efforts or omission of some impor-

---

[21] Judd, Charles H. and Others, *Report of a Survey of the State Institutions of Higher Learning in Indiana*, December, 1926, p. 92.
[22] Capen, Samuel P. and Stevens, Edwin B., *Report of a Survey of the University of Nevada*. Bureau of Education Bulletin (1917) No. 19.

tant aspects. Finally, group responsibility provides an opportunity for those so inclined to shirk their share of the work involved. Such shirking develops ill will and lowers faculty morale. The placing of responsibility directly upon an administrative officer who in turn can divide the total task among his assistants will provide for specialization of abilities and less vacillation in decisions.

Table II, page 11, shows a predominant agreement among the members of the jury of presidents in rating this criterion as highly desirable.

Criterion 19.

Administrative organization should provide for the approval of policies by the state board of control.[23]

The state maintains its control of the teachers college through a board. The president is the chief executive officer of the institution for that board. He must, as long as he remains chief executive, so formulate policies that the board's approval will be forthcoming. Administration without approval of policies may undermine the whole institution. Policies which fail to secure approval of the board of control are probably lacking in clarity of statement and purpose or are unsound. The chief executive who neglects to refer to his board for approval of proposed policies is likely to lessen the board's subsequent support at times when full cooperation and endorsement are highly desirable. Such neglect may ultimately prove disastrous to both the institution and its president.

Table II, page 11, shows that the jury of selected presidents rates this criterion as desirable. Three of the jurors rated it as representing a harmful administrative condition. One president commented: "Board meetings should be devoted to reviewing achievement since the last board meeting. If achievement is sufficiently high, the board will vote confidence to the president and not restrict him with formulated policies."

Criterion 20.

Administrative organization should provide for the making of final decisions by the president after policies have been approved

[23]Rutledge, S. A., *The Development of Guiding Principles for the Administration of Teachers Colleges and Normal Schools*, p. 18. Lindsay, E. E. and Holland, E. O., *College and University Administration*, pp. 20–21. Kent, Raymond A., *Higher Education in America*, pp. 619–624.

by the state board of control. This criterion is not to be interpreted as interfering with the president's delegating to a subordinate officer authority to make decisions.[24]

In the final analysis the chief executive officer is responsible. Neither the faculty nor groups of the faculty can relieve him of this responsibility. The failure of any phase of the institutional program will sooner or later be brought to the president for an explanation and an accounting. He must reserve the right to reverse decisions of committees, the council, or the faculty, if, in his judgment, the decision is dangerous or undesirable at that time. The careful administrator will avoid the necessity for reversing decisions, but the right to do so should be understood by the faculty and by any committee created.

Theisen says: "The principle of giving the chief executive officer a wide range of authority is commonly accepted among careful students of administrations as a cardinal principle."[25] The president cannot delegate this final responsibility. Any functions delegated for performance are still the president's responsibility. He must accept responsibility for the administration of the institution. Staff members may be held responsible by the president, but the public and the board of control will not permit him to shift responsibility through delegation to a subordinate officer.

SUMMARY

1. A majority of the members of the jury of teachers college presidents approves the following characteristics of internal administrative organization:

A. Opportunity for the instructional staff to teach in their respective departments without being overburdened with administrative duties.

B. Faculty participation in formulating policies concerning instruction.

C. Responsibility for the performance of administrative functions centered in individuals.

D. The approval of policies by the state board of control.

[24]Rutledge, S. A., *Development of Guiding Principles for the Administration of Teachers Colleges and Normal Schools*, p. 19. Lindsay, E. E. and Holland, E. O., *College and University Administration*, p. 472. Foster, William T., "Faculty Participation in College Government," *School and Society*, April 22, 1916, p. 597.
[25]Theisen, William W., *The City Superintendent and the Board of Education*, p. 61.

E. Final decisions made by president or by officers to whom president has delegated authority to make decisions.

F. The utilization of an administrative council chosen by the president to serve in an advisory capacity concerning the formulation of policies and the making of administrative decisions.   (Faculty representation on the administrative council received high endorsement.)

G. The freeing of the president from a multiplicity of administrative duties.

H. Grouping of related administrative functions under control of officers who in turn are responsible to president.

I. Specialization of duties of the administrative officers.

J. Special committees for investigations requiring special study.

K. Few or no standing committees for administration of functions.

L. A fixed procedure for replacing membership in standing committees.

M. Selection and appointment of all committees by the president.

2. A majority of the members of the same jury disapproves (1) selection of special and standing committees by faculty or representatives of faculty, and (2) providing of standing committees for administration of all major groups of functions.

3. To a limited extent the jury differentiates because of financial support.   Where support is limited, there is a lower rating for desirability of freeing the president from a multiplicity of duties and for providing for few rather than many administrative committees.   A few comments by jurors will explain the attitude of several concerning financial support:

"I do not believe differing conditions of financial support alter the significance of a criterion.   An institution which lets itself go slack because it is rich may be covering up losses temporarily which represent serious eventual losses.   The poor institution has to use the best administration at all times.   If it has the willingness to do this, it is fortunate."

"I cannot conceive of the policy being very different even though financial support is particularly curtailed."

"I do not see any reason for change in general administrative policies on account of financial support."

"My vote is the same regardless of how limited or curtailed the financial support may be."

CHAPTER III

THE ADMINISTRATIVE USE OF COMMITTEES IN INTERNAL ORGANIZATION IN TEACHERS COLLEGES

WITH the criteria validated and discussed, the succeeding chapters will examine critically the internal administrative organizations found in one hundred and fifty teachers colleges of different sizes. This chapter, dealing with committees, is represented in three sections:

I. The present status of committee organization.
II. Conflicting viewpoints concerning the functions of committees in administration.
III. An analysis of procedures used for administrative control of committees.

I. THE PRESENT STATUS OF COMMITTEE ORGANIZATION

1. *To what extent are standing committees organized in teachers colleges?*

An examination of Table III shows that there are 1451 standing committees now organized in the one hundred and fifty teachers colleges included in this study. In addition to those listed, there were a few standing committees reported which occurred so infrequently that they were not included in the tabulations. This is an average of approximately ten standing committees organized for each of the colleges which furnished data.

Seven of the colleges reported no standing committees. Others reported as many as twenty-two different ones. The average number of standing committees per institution increases as the enrollment grows larger, but even the small colleges average slightly more than eight standing committees.

2. *What standing committees are organized most frequently?*

The entertainment and lyceum committee has the greatest frequency of occurrence. Table III shows that 106 such com-

27

TABLE III

STANDING COMMITTEES ORGANIZED IN 150 TEACHERS COLLEGES IN THE UNITED STATES. 1932

Name of Standing Committee	22 Colleges Enrollment Below 300			68 Colleges Enrollment 300–799			27 Colleges Enrollment 800–1199			33 Colleges Enrollment 1200 and Above			All Colleges Combined		
	Yes	No	% Yes	Yes	No	% Yes	Yes	No	% Yes	Yes	No	% Yes	Yes	No	% Yes
Buildings and grounds	4	18	18.2	12	56	17.6	12	15	44.4	11	22	33	39	111	26.1
Class schedule	10	12	45.4	34	34	50.0	19	8	70.3	13	20	39	76	74	50.7
College publications	9	13	41.0	30	38	44.1	14	13	51.8	24	9	72	77	73	51.4
Curriculum	13	9	59.0	40	28	58.8	19	8	70.3	22	6	81	99	51	66.1
Entertainment and lyceum	14	8	63.6	49	19	72.0	21	6	77.7	22	11	66	106	44	70.7
Entrance and credits	14	8	63.6	33	35	48.5	19	8	70.3	25	8	75	91	59	60.7
Executive	6	16	27.2	26	42	38.2	16	11	59.2	12	21	36	60	90	40.0
Extension and correspondence	5	17	22.7	15	53	22.1	10	17	37.0	15	8	45	45	105	30.0
Library	9	13	41.0	29	39	42.6	14	13	51.8	20	13	60	72	78	48.1
Placement of graduates	12	10	54.5	39	29	57.3	19	8	70.3	20	13	60	90	60	60.0
Public exercises	7	15	31.8	30	38	44.1	11	16	40.7	12	21	36	60	90	40.0
Public relations	1	21	4.5	6	62	8.8	4	23	14.8	2	31	6	13	137	8.7
Registration	10	12	45.4	29	39	42.6	14	13	51.8	19	14	57	72	78	48.1
Scholarship and loans	11	11	50.0	44	24	64.7	14	13	51.8	26	7	78	95	55	63.4
Student activities	14	8	63.6	48	20	70.6	18	9	66.6	24	9	72	104	46	69.4
Student employment	6	16	27.2	23	45	33.8	13	14	48.1	14	19	42	56	94	37.4
Student publications	9	13	41.0	42	26	61.7	18	9	66.6	25	8	75	94	56	62.8
Student social affairs	12	10	54.5	51	17	75.0	17	10	62.9	23	10	69	103	47	68.7
Student welfare	11	11	50.0	26	42	38.2	8	19	29.6	15	18	45	60	90	40.0
Training school	6	16	27.2	15	53	22.1	9	18	33.3	9	24	27	39	111	26.1
Total	183			621			289			353			1451		
Average per college	8.3			9.1			10.7			10.8			9.7		

This table should be read as follows: In 22 colleges with enrollment below 300 students, there are 4 colleges or 18.2% which have a buildings and grounds committee and 18 with no such committee, etc.

mittees are organized in approximately 70 per cent of the colleges reporting. The prevalence of this committee is slightly greater in the large and extra large institutions. In frequency of occurrence committees which concern student activities, student social affairs, and the curriculum rank second, third, and fourth respectively. Other committees found in more than half of the institutions are, in the order of their frequency of occurrence, the committees with the following titles: scholarship and loans, student publications, entrance and credits, placement of graduates, college publications, and class schedule. The striking thing about these committees with a high frequency of occurrence is that, with the exception of the curriculum committee, they deal largely with student personnel management. There are relatively few committees concerned with matters of instruction, finance, or public relations.

3. *What differences concerning frequency of occurrence of standing committees are found in small, medium, large, and extra large colleges?**

Committees are organized with a higher frequency in colleges enrolling more than 800 students than in those institutions enrolling fewer than that number. There are six committees whose frequency of occurrence generally increases as the enrollment increases. These committees are those dealing with the functions of college publications, curriculum, extension and correspondence, library, placement of graduates, and student publications. There are no committees which generally decrease in frequency of occurrence from the small to the extra large colleges. However, there is one committee, that which deals with student welfare, which is found in half of the small colleges but occurs less frequently in colleges with medium, large, or extra large enrollments.

Percentages of organized committees vary greatly in large and extra large colleges. The percentage of class schedule committees in large colleges is nearly twice as great as that which occurs in colleges enrolling above 1200 students. A second marked difference is evident concerning college publications committees. There are approximately three such committees in extra large colleges to two in colleges with between 800 and

*These terms are used in this study for the following college enrollments: enrollment below 300; enrollment 300–799; enrollment 800–1199; enrollment 1200 and above.

1199 students.   A third marked difference occurs regarding the scholarship and loans committees.   There is a decidedly higher percentage of these committees in the extra large colleges.   A fourth difference is noted in institutions enrolling under 800 students. These colleges have a much smaller percentage of extension and correspondence study committees.

4. *Do presidents have administrative councils in teachers colleges?*

An administrative council is reported in 70 per cent of the colleges responding.   Table IV shows the frequency with which

TABLE IV

Types of Organization Used in the Administrative Councils Found in 150 Teachers Colleges.   1932

Organization Type	22 Colleges Enrollment Under 300 8 Councils		68 Colleges Enrollment 300–799 50 Councils		27 Colleges Enrollment 800–1199 18 Councils		33 Colleges Enrollment 1200 or Above 30 Councils		All Colleges Combined 106 Councils	
	f	%	f	%	f	%	f	%	f	%
None...............	14	63.6	18	26.5	9	33.3	3	9	44	29.4
Department heads....	0	0	6	8.8	2	7.4	6	18	14	9.4
Department heads and administrative officers...............	1	4.5	0	0	4	14.8	3	9	8	5.4
All major administrative officers........	0	0	0	0	0	0	6	18	6	4.1
Appointees of the president.............	7	31.8	39	57.3	12	44.4	13	39	71	47.4
Representatives of faculty..............	0	0	4	5.9	0	0	1	3	5	3.4
Administrative officers and faculty representatives.........	0	0	1	1.5	0	0	1	3	2	1.4

This table should be read as follows: In 22 colleges with enrollment under 300 there are 14 which have no administrative council, 1 council made up of department heads, 7 councils consisting of appointees of the presidents, etc.

such councils occur in the colleges of different sizes.   It also shows how these councils are chosen.   Approximately one-third of the small institutions have councils, while in the extra large colleges there are 90 per cent with councils.   In institutions of all sizes the prevailing method for choosing the council is by presidential appointment.   A few councils are made up of department heads. Eight councils consist of department heads and administrative officers. Six institutions have councils made up of administrative officers only. Five councils are composed of representatives of the faculty.

Two comments by presidents who furnished data for the study give interesting viewpoints concerning administrative councils. The president of one small college wrote: "Our staff is small; hence the entire group serves as an administrative council." Another president reported as follows: "The administrative council represents all the departments and activities of the college, and serves the following purposes: (*a*) considers points of strength and points of weakness in college organization and procedures, (*b*) discusses policies as introduced by the president and dean of instruction, (*c*) assists in the formulation of policies relative to college organization and instruction, (*d*) introduces departmental problems for discussion, (*e*) recommends policies affecting general organization and instruction, (*f*) serves as a clearing house for various problems which might otherwise come directly to the general staff meetings, (*g*) is the principal advisory, promotional, and unifying influence in the life of the college, (*h*) reaches through its representation every department and every staff member and promotes through departmental meetings and committees whatever policies or procedures have been passed upon by the council."

5. *What factors in teachers colleges correlate positively or negatively with the number of committees organized in each institution?*

Data which the writer believes comparable and computed on the same basis were secured in 130 institutions and correlated. The data reported by twenty institutions were not included in the correlations because of a different basis for computing totals. Some of the twenty institutions not included reported enrollments as gross totals. That is, the total enrollments for each term were added and the sum reported as the enrollment for the institution. Such reports might include one student three times in the gross total. Other institutions included training school enrollments in their totals. Some financial reports were not comparable because gross receipts from book store sales, athletic contests, and dormitories were included as financial support. Only those institutions whose attendance and financial data were comparable were included in the statistical correlations.

The product moment formula was used to compute the co-efficients of correlation between the number of committees per institution and five other variables as follows: (1) the number of administrative officers per institution, (2) the college enrollment, (3) financial support per student in attendance, (4) the length of tenure of the president, and (5) the average number of hours taught per week by the administrative officers within the colleges.   The coefficients of correlation are as follows:

A. Number of committees and number of administrative officers per institution: $r = 0.2854 \pm .0543$.

B. Number of committees per institution and number of students enrolled per institution: $r = 0.1358 \pm .0581$.

C. Number of committees per institution and financial support per student per institution: $r = 0.1135 \pm .0584$.

D. Number of committees per institution and the length of the president's tenure: $r = 0.0670 \pm .0589$.

E. Number of committees per institution and the average number of hours taught per week by administrative officers: $r = 0.1605 \pm .0576$.

These correlations were computed in an attempt to throw light on the following questions:

A. Do teachers colleges with a large number of administrative officers have a correspondingly large number of committees?

B. Is a college with a large enrollment likely to have a large number of committees?

C. Will colleges with liberal financial support have more or fewer committees than those with limited support?

D. Do presidents with long tenure of service usually have few or many committees?

E. Do administrative officers teach more or fewer hours per week in colleges having a large number of committees?

The coefficients of correlation reported above are not high enough to indicate definite relationships which might answer the questions raised.   The coefficient of correlation between the number of committees and the number of administrative officers is 0.2854 ± .0543. This is in all probability a true correlation better than zero and indicates that a teachers college with a large number of committees will probably have a large number of administrative officers. The correlation is too low to expect a close correspondence and we may expect to find some institutions with few committees and many administrative officers. It does, however, cast doubt on the assumption that institutions with few administrative officers have a large number of committees to administer the functions usually performed by officers. Since the other coefficients of correlation are all less than four times their probable error, it is unsafe to say that the correlations as found indicate that the number of committees in an institution is significantly related to enrollment, financial support, or length of the president's tenure; and neither is the average teaching load of administrative assistants closely related to the number of committees in the institution.

II. CONFLICTING VIEWPOINTS CONCERNING THE FUNCTIONS OF COMMITTEES IN ADMINISTRATION

There are two conflicting viewpoints concerning the administrative use of committees. The one viewpoint contends that the chief function of committees is to study problems and recommend policies, not to carry the routine of administrative duties. Those holding this viewpoint would place the administrative control of all functions in the hands of regular executive officers and leave the professorial staff free to teach in their various departments. This viewpoint is well stated by Agnew,[1] who lists as one of his guiding principles the following: "The chief duty of faculty committees is to study problems and recommend policies, not to carry the routine of executive duties. The latter should be in the hands of regular executive officers, leaving the professional staff free to exercise the teaching function." In the written discussion which precedes the statement of this principle, Agnew makes it very clear that he believes in staff participation in framing the policies of the institution. In part he says[2]: "The teaching staff of the professional school should participate in framing the policies of the institution.

[1]Agnew, Walter D., *The Administration of the Professional School for Teachers*, p. 257.
[2]*Ibid.*

Such participation gives to the staff an adequate knowledge of administrative problems, it secures proper cooperation and discovers the powers, the aptitudes, and capacities of many who would otherwise remain in obscurity with valuable talents unemployed." A careful reading of Agnew's study leads to the conclusion that the staff participation which he recommends would be realized through membership in special committees.

Agnew, by advocating the above principle, stands in opposition to administration through committees. He infers that committees, because of special capacities of their members, have a contribution to make in policy formation. The use of these special talents is a move toward efficiency and not necessarily toward democracy.

Reeves and Russell,[3] after studying the organization and administration of the colleges under the control of the Disciples of Christ Church, state: "The writers are very doubtful as to the worth of faculty committees for administrative purposes. Most of the committees represented are administrative in their nature. The work attempted by these committees would be better performed if given to responsible individuals. Individuals are more likely to specialize their knowledge and less likely to vacillate in their decisions. When administrative functions are performed by individuals, the responsibility for decisions is more easily placed and the source of decisions is more quickly located by everyone concerned. Lastly, the valuable time of many faculty members is conserved."

A further viewpoint is expressed by Evenden,[4] writing on the improvement of college teaching: "An increased amount of faculty participation in determining school policies which affect instruction will undoubtedly bring about a better understanding of the program for the entire college and of the work of other departments, and will prevent undesirable duplications in instructional materials and promote a higher degree of cooperation among the teachers. The present tendency for college instructors to ask for and receive a greater share of responsibility in the general administration of college affairs will work against the improvement of instruction unless the responsibility is confined to issues quite definitely related to the content and methods of

[3]Reeves, Floyd W. and Russell, John Dale, *College Organization and Administration*, p. 75.
[4]Evenden, E. S., "The Improvement of College Teaching," *Teachers College Record*, April, 1928, pp. 587–596.

instruction, the arrangement of courses, and similar questions. College administration requires special abilities and demands special training. Successful college administrators must continue to study and conduct research in the field of their responsibilities just as certainly as college teachers must in their fields. Because these fields are very different, however, to ask specialists in subject-matter fields to cast intelligent votes on matters of general administration is to ask them to keep up in two fields instead of one with the resultant neglect of both." This is a strong statement which restricts the faculty to matters of instruction and by so doing places the administration of functions as the responsibility of executive officials and not in the hands of committees charged with administrative responsibilities.

The conflicting viewpoint is upheld by Sherrod[5], who recommends that presidents delegate the administrative functions of their institutions to a group of eighteen committees with legislative and administrative functions delegated to each. In his discussion introducing the problem of administration through committees, Sherrod states: "The duties of an administrator in charge of an educational institution have become so numerous and technical that he has been forced to resort to his faculty for relief."[6]

Few people will deny that administrative duties in teachers colleges are numerous and technical, but the question naturally arises whether or not it is good administration to turn to the faculty for relief. The history of the development of educational administration in normal schools and teachers colleges shows that administration has developed for the purpose of expediting and improving the work of the classroom instructor.

Administration must provide for rendering services. The efficiency and adequacy of the services rendered justify to a large extent the expenditure of time, money, and energy in administration. Sherrod's statement quoted above can be interpreted as based upon two assumptions. The first of these is that the administrative duties of the president are primary and teaching by the faculty secondary. Calling the faculty to perform administrative duties is bound to reduce the energy and

[5]Sherrod, C. C., *The Administration of State Teachers Colleges Through Faculty Committees*, p. 75.
[6]*Ibid.*, p. 7.

time which might be used in classroom instruction, unless the teaching load is reduced accordingly. If such a reduction is made, it should be as easy to provide administrative officers to whom the president can "turn for relief" as it is to provide additional faculty members to take up the teaching load from which the members of the committees are relieved.

The second assumption is that faculty committees are capable of rendering technical service. If presidents are forced to turn to their faculties because administrative duties are technical, then technical service is expected. Further evidence that Sherrod assumes faculty committees capable of rendering expert administrative service is found in his discussion of the principle of delegating administrative authority. He quotes from Theisen as follows: "We are taught then that the form of administration which makes for efficiency is one that is centralized or coordinated. It is the one in which professional leadership is recognized and in which executive functions are assigned to experts."[7]

Sherrod uses this statement by Theisen in contending that duties should be assigned to committees and authority delegated to them. In so doing he must assume that members of committees are expert administrators, but no evidence is given to prove that they are. In fact he gives evidence to the contrary. His investigation of committee service in teachers colleges led him to make the following statement: "Committees as a rule have no regular time of meeting, keep no records of their activities and make no written report to the president or to the faculty. They meet rather seldom and then at the call of the chairman. Some committees have not had meetings in months and a few have had no meetings in a year or more."[8]

These findings by Sherrod show that committee members are not expert administrators nor eager to learn how to become expert through committee participation.

These two viewpoints as discussed are definitely opposed. The first, advocated by Agnew, Reeves, Russell, and Evenden, would use committees to investigate special topics involving research and time which need not be duplicated by all faculty

[7]Theisen, W. W., *The City Superintendent and the Board of Education*, p. 100.
[8]Sherrod, C. C., *The Administration of State Teachers Colleges Through Faculty Committees*, p. 34.

members, and to formulate policies regarding instruction. The second viewpoint, advocated by Sherrod, would use committees as legislative and administrative bodies. It seems reasonable to interpret such use of committees as based upon an assumption that administrative duties are primary and classroom teaching is secondary. Such use of committees also assumes that committee members are or will become expert administrators to whom presidents can assign technical duties for administrative performance.

III. AN ANALYSIS OF PROCEDURES USED FOR ADMINISTRATIVE CONTROL OF COMMITTEES

An analysis of Table V shows the prevalence of procedures used in the administrative control of committees in teachers colleges. This table was compiled from detailed data summarized concerning the procedures used in controlling each committee listed in Table III, page 28. These summaries show that procedures within an institution are the same for all committees. If the president appointed one committee, he appointed all others. If one committee reported in writing, all committees for that institution reported in writing. If the president were ex-officio a member of one committee in the institution over which he presided, he was ex-officio a member of all other committees in that institution. Hence this analysis will concern all committees within an institution, and not separate and distinct committees. The purpose of this section of this chapter is to analyze the procedure in the various colleges used in control of committees. In this analysis specific questions are discussed.

1. *Are committees appointed by the president?*

In approximately 90 per cent of the institutions investigated committees are appointed by the president. Committees appointed in this manner feel responsible to him. It is probably safe to assume that on the whole the president knows the specific abilities of faculty members better than any other individual or group of individuals in the institution. He would also be familiar with the amount of time each faculty member could reasonably be expected to devote to committee service. This knowledge should enable the president to appoint committees which will include the best talent in the institution. Since in the final analysis the president is responsible for the actions of all committees in the institution under his control, it is natural for him to make appointments.

2. *Do any presidents permit the faculty to select committees?*

Only a few of the presidents permit their faculties to select committees. There are some who contend that faculties should name their own committees. Such a viewpoint overlooks the fact that the committee is needed for a specific task and not to represent the faculty. One president in responding to this question stated: "Appointment of committees by faculty action has two serious disadvantages. First, popular members of the staff will be selected regardless of ability or time available to perform the task involved by appointment to the committees. Second, committee members chosen by the faculty oftentimes feel that they represent a faction, group, or department within the staff. Such comments as 'Miss Jones will represent the women well; I suggest her for membership in the committee,' or 'The history department has not had a committee chairman for some time; I nominate Mr. Brown,' show definitely how choice of committees by the faculty may aggravate jealousy and interfere with efficiency."

3. *Is the president ex-officio a member of committees?*

A large percentage of presidents report that they are ex-officio members of all committees in the institution over which they preside. Seventy-five per cent of the presidents included in this investigation follow this procedure. It is a means of keeping in close contact with all committee activities. However, the president who serves on a committee is likely to dominate the situation from the beginning and not get the best thinking or initiative of the individual committeeman. If many committees are appointed for investigations, ex-officio membership, if taken seriously by the president, may mean an overburdening of his time which might well be spent otherwise. Those committees in which presidents most frequently retain a membership are those concerning the curriculum, entrance and credits, and the training school.

4. *Do committees make investigations?*

There are, according to the reports made by the presidents who furnished data for this study, 1141 committees in the 150 institutions who make investigations. This is approximately 80 per cent of the total number of committees organized. Any individual or group working to formulate policies or to administer them needs facts as the basis for decisions. Committees are justified when the work required for the investigation necessary for getting facts is too heavy or too complex for one individual. Other situations justifying committees are those which require several points of view or group judgment in formulating policies. Those committees which make no investigations probably do not function or make their decisions without investigating the data pertinent to the situation. Committees which are reported most frequently as not making investigations are those dealing with entrance and credits, public exercises, scholarships, and student social affairs.

5. *Do committees make recommendations?*

Recommendations are natural results of committee organization. Table V shows that 93 per cent of the committees organized do make recommendations. On the other hand the same table shows that but 79 per cent of these committees make investigations. This indicates that 14 per cent of all committees may make recommendations without first investigating. A further indication is that recommendations may be made in some institutions without any organized effort to supplement group thinking with facts which are pertinent to the problem.

6. *Do committees initiate policies through legislation?*

Nearly half of all committees initiate policies through legislation. This is the only procedure concerning which practice is about evenly divided. The percentage of committees which initiate policies is fairly constant for institutions of various sizes. The original data show that the curriculum, executive, and student activity committees initiate policies more frequently than others. In colleges enrolling over 1200 students, the library, placement, and training school committees initiate policies in a high percentage of the institutions. Several differences, apparently due to variations in enrollment, appear in the original data.　The percentage of training school committees having power to initiate policies becomes higher as colleges increase in enrollment.　Fewer student employment committees have power to initiate through legislation as institutions grow larger.　Student activity committees initiate policies in a greater percentage of the large institutions than of the small.

7. *Do committees administer policies?*

Table V reveals that 78 per cent of the 1451 committees reported in this study administer policies.　Since only 45 per cent of the committees initiate policies by legislation, approximately half of the committees which administer policies must have them initiated by some other authority.　Apparently many presidents depend upon committees to administer policies but reserve the right to initiate such policies as they think desirable.　By reserving the authority to initiate policies, presidents provide a means for stopping any committee action which may be undesirable.　One president wrote: "Organization of committees is primarily for the purpose of recommending policies and programs, and the administrative functions are entirely divorced from the work of the standing committee unless delegated and assigned after the chief executive officer passes upon the recommendation."

Data previously presented in this chapter pointed out that there are on the average ten committees for each teachers college.　Since a large percentage of them administers policies, opportunities for conflicts between committee members and administrative officers must occur.　Unless committees and officers have separate and distinct duties in the administration of functions, responsibility for their performance will be difficult to place.　Performance of routine administration consumes time which might be used for investigation and teaching.　Such performance forces members of administrative committees to keep up in two fields, instruction and administration, with the probable neglect of both.

8. *May the president reverse decisions of committees?*

Approximately 80 per cent of the committees make decisions which may be reversed by the president.　Since the president cannot shift his responsibility to the committee making the

TABLE V

PREVALENCE OF PROCEDURES USED IN ADMINISTRATIVE CONTROL OF COMMITTEES IN 150 TEACHERS COLLEGES. 1932

Questions Indicating Procedures Used in Administration of Committees	22 Colleges Enrollment Under 300 N = 183			68 Colleges Enrollment 300–799 N = 621			27 Colleges Enrollment 800–1199 N = 289			33 Colleges Enrollment 1200 or Above N = 358			All Colleges Combined N = 1451		
	Yes	No	% Yes	Yes	No	% Yes	Yes	No	% Yes	Yes	No	% Yes	Yes	No	% Yes
1. Are committees appointed by the president?	173	10	94.5	558	65	89.8	271	18	93.8	315	43	88.0	1317	134	90.8
2. Are committees selected by the faculty?	5	178	2.7	44	577	7.1	18	271	6.2	37	321	10.3	104	1347	7.2
3. Is the president ex-officio a member of committees?	162	21	88.5	454	167	73.1	243	46	84.1	221	137	61.7	1080	371	74.4
4. Do committees make investigations?	133	50	72.7	457	164	71.9	251	38	86.8	300	58	83.8	1141	310	78.6
5. Do committees make recommendations?	176	7	96.7	566	55	91.1	276	13	95.5	335	23	93.6	1353	98	93.2
6. Do committees initiate policies through legislation?	85	98	46.4	261	360	42.0	128	161	44.3	173	185	48.3	647	804	44.6
7. Do committees administer policies?	138	45	75.4	425	196	68.4	270	19	93.4	291	67	81.3	1124	327	77.5
8. May the president reverse decisions of committees?	157	26	85.8	401	220	64.6	269	20	93.1	319	39	89.1	1146	305	78.9
9. Is there a regular way to replace members of committees?	126	57	68.9	420	201	67.6	243	46	84.1	328	30	91.6	1117	334	76.9
10. Is there a tendency to retain the same individuals on committees?	161	22	87.9	490	131	78.9	258	31	89.2	310	48	86.6	1219	232	84.0
11. Do committees have written lists of duties?	44	139	24.0	147	474	23.6	77	212	26.6	106	252	29.6	374	1077	25.8
12. Do committees report in writing?	100	83	54.6	269	352	43.3	173	116	59.8	216	142	60.3	758	693	52.2
13. Are there usually some administrative officers on committees?	159	24	86.9	387	234	62.3	210	79	72.7	293	65	81.8	1049	402	72.3
14. Do committees function each year?	168	15	91.8	559	62	90.0	281	8	97.2	344	14	96.1	1352	99	93.2

This table should be read as follows: In 22 colleges with enrollment under 300 there are 183 committees. The presidents appointed 173 of these committees. Five committees were appointed by the faculty, etc. In a few colleges committees are selected by, the executive council committee on committees, or by a state director of teacher training.

decisions, this leaves little control to the president in those institutions in which he may not reverse committee decisions. Since 90 per cent of the committees are appointed by the president and since 80 per cent of the committees may have their decisions reversed, there are some institutions in which the power to appoint committees does not carry with it authority to reverse their decisions if such reversal is thought desirable. Some comments will contribute to an understanding of this phase of committee control. One president wrote: "We never talk about reversing committee decisions. All of our committees understand that recommendations must be approved before any action is undertaken. Any committee recommendation thought dangerous or unwise is filed for further consideration. No action can occur until approval. Hence reversal of decision is not necessary." This procedure takes care of the situation unless action must be taken which is opposite to the committee recommendation. If opposite action is taken under the approval of the president, even though the committee recommendation is "filed for further consideration," the members of the committee know that their decision has been reversed.

Another president commented: "Reversal of a committee decision is likely to destroy cooperation and initiative. I shall reverse decisions as a last resort. Thus far, I have followed the plan of meeting with the committee whose decision seemed dangerous or unwise. In every case the committee, upon considering data which I presented, reversed its own decision."

9. *Is there a regular way to replace members of committees?*

Provision is made for the replacement of members in 77 per cent of the committees reported in this study. Some of the reasons for needing to replace members in a committee are very obvious. Those who neglect to do their share should be removed. When a lack of harmony interferes with committee efficiency, removal of one or more members may be necessary. Sometimes a member of a committee will have an unexpected increase in his academic and extra-curricular load; it would seem in such circumstances that the wise procedure would be to lighten the total load by removal from committee membership. Several comments were made by presidents concerning procedures used. One president said: "Since I appoint all committees, I feel free to remove any or all members whenever it seems wise." Another plan advocated and used is to limit the total time any one individual can serve on a standing committee. Two presidents commented that they do not permit any staff member to serve on any standing committee more than two consecutive years. Several others stated that committees are all discontinued at the end of each academic year, and new ones appointed at the beginning of the new year. Larger institutions have provided a regular way to replace committee members in a higher percentage of cases than the smaller colleges. One president wrote: "Some standing committees should have a constant personnel. Others are better if changed frequently."

10. *Is there a tendency to retain the same individuals on committees?*

In institutions of all sizes there is a high percentage of presidents who report that they tend to keep the same individuals on committees. In the 150 colleges investigated, this tendency is reported for 84 per cent of the committees. If committees are to administer policies, this tendency is probably one way to gain efficiency in administration. A concrete example will illustrate this contention. A committee administering the registration and classification of students will learn how to carry on registration by actually doing it. Every time new members are put on the committee it will be necessary for them to go through a period of trial and error in registration. However, such a committee will be hard to hold responsible as a group. The chairman will probably become the registrar. He may be able to get some assistance from other members of his committee. If the committee is to function by making investigations, it seems reasonable to assume that new members will add new enthusiasm and new ideas for consideration in policies to be recommended.

11. *Do committees have written lists of duties?*

Approximately one committee in four is given a written list of duties. This indicates that the majority of teachers college presidents considers it desirable for committees to define their own functions and proceed as they deem best. Such a policy may have at least two negative results.   Committees without a written list of duties may not attempt to function.   On the other hand, they may spend a great deal of valuable time in discussion trying to determine just what functions they are to perform.   A second negative result may occur when a committee without a written list of duties proceeds to function in a way not intended by the president who created the committee. Such activity is likely to waste valuable time and energy and the lack of a written assignment of duties makes it impossible for the president to hold the committee chairman, or members of the committee, responsible.   It is quite evident that a written list of duties will restrict a committee in its scope of activities. One president reported, "Committees need to be definitely restricted by a written list of duties.   I know an institution where the chairman of the curriculum committee assumed functions in the assignment of instructors to teach courses.   Conflict between the committee and department heads resulted. As a result no constructive work was done on the curriculum for over a year.   A carefully written assignment of duties would have prevented this conflict."

12. *Do committees report in writing?*

Table V, page 41, shows that more than half of the committees do report in writing.   The majority is so small that the practice cannot be said to be well established.   It seems reasonable to assume that reports would be more carefully made if written.   Since 93 per cent of the committees make recommendations, it would seem that written reports would be made by a percentage of institutions equally as large.   However, Table V, page 41, shows that approximately 40 per cent of the committees make recommendations without making written reports. The original data show that such practice is not limited to small institutions.   Seven out of the twenty-seven curriculum committees in teachers colleges enrolling 1200 or more students do not submit written reports.   The lack of such reports from the curriculum committee may greatly reduce the effectiveness of the committee's recommendations.   It seems reasonable to assume that any committee recommendation would be more clearly understood if based upon written reports. Administration of the functions involved in committee recommendations would be more effective if written reports were available for reference.

13. *Are there usually some administrative officers on committees?*

This question was answered in the affirmative for 72 per cent of the committees reported. This is evidence that practically three-fourths of the committees are partially made up of executive officers. These officials usually have information which is fundamental for the committee's consideration of its problem. For that reason, it seems safe to assume that an administrative officer aided by other staff members would constitute a satisfactory personnel for a committee whose function it is to make an investigation or to formulate policies. On the other hand, such a committee, if charged with administrative functions, may have two undesirable aspects. First, aggressive members of the committee may interfere with the executive officer's performance of his duties. Second, an executive officer who shares the responsibility of his duties with other members of a committee cannot be held entirely responsible for the efficient performance of the functions of his office.

14. *Do committees function each year?*

Presidents of one hundred and fifty teachers colleges reported that 1352 standing committees function each year. No evidence was collected to indicate just what is meant by the functioning of a committee. However, the fact that 7 per cent of the committees were reported as not functioning may indicate that a greater percentage was not functioning with a high degree of efficiency. The non-functioning of committees may be partially explained by data in Table V, page 41, which show that only 25 per cent of committees have a written list of duties, and that nearly half of them are not held for written reports.

IV. SUMMARY

1. Standing committees are organized in teachers colleges of all sizes, with the number of committees increasing as the enrollment increases.

2. The average number of committees for each teachers college is approximately ten.

3. Committees reported most frequently are those dealing with the following: (1) entertainment and lyceum, (2) student activities, (3) student social affairs, and (4) curriculum.

4. There are six committees whose percentage of frequency increases as the enrollment becomes larger.   These committees deal with the following: (1) college publications, (2) curriculum, (3) extension and correspondence, (4) library, (5) placement of graduates, and (6) student publications.

5. The student welfare committee occurs less frequently as colleges become larger.

6. Administrative councils are reported in 70 per cent of the teachers colleges.

7. Members of administrative councils are usually appointed by the president.

8. There are two viewpoints concerning functions of committees in teachers colleges as follows:

A. One viewpoint restricts committee functions to making investigations and formulating policies.

B. A second viewpoint broadens the functions of committees to include the authority to legislate and to administer.

9. The following practices are predominatingly prevalent in the administrative control of committees:

A. Presidents usually appoint committees.

B. In a few institutions the faculty selects committees.

C. The president retains membership in the majority of committees.

D. Committees are used to investigate, to recommend policies, to legislate, and to administer.

E. Presidents retain the right to reverse decisions of committees.

F. In a majority of colleges there is a regular way to replace members of committees.

G. Presidents tend to keep the same individuals on committees.

H. Committees on the whole are not given written lists of duties, nor do they report in writing.

I. There are usually some administrative officers on committees.

J. Presidents report that committees function regularly.

V. CRITICAL EVALUATION

1. Table II, page 11, shows that expert administrators are in almost unanimous agreement that administrative organization should provide opportunity for the instructional staff to teach without being overburdened with administrative duties. An institutional average of ten committees serving largely to administer functions is evidence that administrative organization in many institutions contributes to the burden of the instructional staff. If these administrative functions which are performed by committees are such that group judgment is necessary for their successful administration, or if the burden is such that one individual cannot carry it alone, then committees may be justified. For the administration of those duties which are routine in nature committee organization forces inconvenience upon the members. They must find a time when they can get together; they must agree upon details of performance; they often duplicate each other's efforts. If the work is parceled out to various members, there is often delay because one member did not complete his task in time. If the work is faulty, it is almost impossible to fix responsibility on any individual. It seems reasonable to assume that delegating functions to individuals for administration will save time, fix responsibility, and thereby promote efficiency.

2. Special committees to make investigations requiring special study are rated as highly desirable. The very fact that they are to investigate a special topic means that their work is delimited. They have an idea of what to do. An investigation by a special committee is a task which can be finished, and this in itself is an incentive for action rather than for delay. Since these special committees are charged with making investigations which require special study, the motivation for effort will come out of the investigation itself. Further, if committees are limited to those investigations which require special study, the number of committees will thereby be reduced. Still further, such limitation forces the administrator to decide what investigations need special study before appointing a committee. Thus the criterion calls for special consideration and study by the president before passing the responsibility to a group of his staff members.

3. An administrative council appointed by the president is rated as highly desirable by the jury of experts. This rating justifies the predominant practice found in the colleges investigated. These councils should help presidents in formulating policies and in making administrative decisions. The use of a council rather than the faculty as a whole saves the time of a majority of staff members. An administrative council, if its membership is carefully chosen, should give a well-balanced viewpoint concerning how a new policy would affect every phase of the institution. The council approved by the jury is an advisory body. This means that such a council does not make final decisions by a majority vote. It will advise, point out the strength and weakness of any proposal, and help the president see his problem from all possible angles; but it will never make decisions. The making of an administrative decision is the function of the president or an officer to whom he has delegated authority. The responsibility for the decision made cannot be assumed by the council. When administrative councils usurp the prerogative of administrative officers to make decisions, they lose their usefulness and are probably more harmful than useful.

4. Table II, page 11, shows that although a majority of the jury of teachers college presidents favors keeping membership and chairmanship of a committee constant, they also favor a regular way of changing membership in a committee. Predominant practice in the institutions investigated agrees with the jury rating of these criteria. A fixed procedure for replacing committees is desirable when changes are needed. It seems reasonable to assume that changes through a fixed procedure would be less likely to destroy morale than unusual and abrupt changes which might be necessary if there were no fixed procedure. Those few instances in which the retention of a member on a committee seems desirable could probably be met by making exceptions to the regular replacement procedure.

Keeping membership and chairmanship constant may train individuals to perform their tasks better. On the other hand, constant membership or chairmanship may result in a continuance of mediocrity. New members in the committee, or a change in the chairmanship, may stimulate more effort and more efficiency. It is probably safe to say that the best of administrative criteria needs to be used with discrimination, and occasional exceptions must be made to meet the emergencies and needs which develop in local situations.

5. Twenty-eight of the thirty members of the jury agree that presidents should make final decisions after policies have been approved by the board of control. One way in which administrative organization provides for this making of final decisions is the reservation by the president of the right to reverse decisions of committees. As previously pointed out, committee decisions are reversed as a last resort. However, any organization which fails to have its committees understand that their decisions are tentative and subject to administrative reversal leaves itself in a position which invites trouble.

CHAPTER IV

THE INTERRELATIONS OF ADMINISTRATIVE OFFICERS

IT IS assumed that the relationships which are established between and among the various administrative officers within a teachers college do much toward fixing responsibility, stimulating leadership in the performance of functional duties, and integrating the entire institutional program. Hence this chapter is an inquiry into these relationships. Criteria, validated by a jury of teachers college presidents, were stated in Chapter II. It is the purpose of this chapter to discuss, in the light of these criteria, the relations which were revealed in the administrative organizations of the 150 teachers colleges included in the investigation described in Chapter I. Stated in another way, the purpose is to show how teachers college presidents have organized their staffs for performing functions of administration.

The discussion will center around the officers usually found in teachers colleges. The following specific questions will be answered:

1. With what frequency are various administrative officers found in teachers colleges of different sizes?
2. How many hours per week do these officers teach in the classroom?
3. What instructional departments are headed by the different administrative officers?
4. To whom are the various officers administratively responsible?

Such a discussion will show the interrelations of officers in teachers colleges. Predominant practices and innovations will be noted. Summaries for institutions of different sizes will be presented in tabular form in this chapter to the end that any differences in procedure which may characterize small, medium sized, large, or extra large institutions may be compared and contrasted.   Finally, a summary and critical evaluation of interrelationships found in internal organizations will be given.

I. BUSINESS AGENTS

An inspection of Table VI shows that four different business officers are included in many of the administrative organizations of the various teachers colleges.   These officers are the business manager, the bursar, the chief accountant, and the chief store-keeper.   Since a check of the original data shows that only a small percentage of the colleges has both a business manager and a bursar, it is practical to combine the data for these two officers and treat the combined data as descriptive of the business agent of the teachers college.   This means that practically 70 per cent of all the institutions have a business agent whose title is either business manager or bursar.   Table VII, page 53, shows that the business agent does not teach.   Neither does the chief accountant nor the chief storekeeper carry any instructional load.   The business agent is found more frequently in the larger colleges.   The original data show that those institutions not having a business agent have their business transacted by either the president or a representative of the state department of education.

The interrelations of the business agent with other officers is shown in Table VIII, page 54.   In no case, in the 150 colleges reported, is the business agent also head of an instructional department.   About one-third of the business agents in this study hold other administrative offices.   In fourteen institutions the business agent is also registrar.   In nine others the office of business agent and the office of chief accountant are combined under the administrative direction of one official.   In six colleges the secretary-treasurer performs the functions of the office of business agent.   In five other institutions the business agent is the superintendent of buildings and grounds.

One would naturally expect to find business agents in the large and extra large colleges holding fewer combination administrative offices than the business agents in smaller colleges. Such is not the case.   Nine of the large colleges and twelve of the extra large colleges have business agents who hold other offices.   These are greater percentages than in the colleges of other sizes.   In 103 cases the business agent is directly responsible to the president.   In one single case the business agent is responsible to the board of trustees and not to the president.

TABLE VI

OFFICERS USED IN THE INTERNAL ADMINISTRATIVE ORGANIZATIONS OF 150
TEACHERS COLLEGES.   1932

Titles of Administrative Officers	22 Colleges Enrollment Under 300		68 Colleges Enrollment 300–799		27 Colleges Enrollment 800–1199		33 Colleges Enrollment 1200 or Above		All Colleges Combined	
	f	%	*f*	%	*f*	%	*f*	%	*f*	%
Business manager..	3	13.6	27	39.7	11	40.7	21	63	62	41.3
Bursar............	4	18.2	17	25.0	10	37.0	11	33	42	28.0
Chief accountant..	5	22.7	26	38.2	11	40.7	16	48	58	38.7
Chief storekeeper..	5	22.7	16	23.5	9	33.3	13	39	43	28.7
Dean of college....	7	31.8	35	51.5	16	59.2	22	66	80	53.4
Dean of men......	8	36.3	37	54.4	17	62.9	23	69	85	56.7
Dean of women....	18	81.7	54	79.4	25	92.5	30	90	127	84.8
Dir. of adjustment.	0	0	6	8.8	2	7.4	6	18	14	9.4
Dir. of athletics....	15	68.1	62	91.1	23	85.1	31	93	131	87.4
Dir. of extension...	7	31.8	25	36.8	14	51.8	23	69	69	46.0
Dir. of health......	8	36.3	44	64.7	18	66.6	25	75	95	63.4
Dir. of housing....	4	18.2	12	17.6	7	25.9	6	18	29	19.4
Dir. of instruction..	3	13.6	5	7.5	3	11.1	6	18	17	11.4
Dir. of personnel...	0	0	5	7.5	0	0	7	21	12	8.0
Dir. of placement..	7	31.8	33	48.5	14	51.8	27	81	81	54.0
Dir. of research....	0	0	12	17.6	4	14.8	11	33	27	18.0
Dir. of student activities..........	4	18.2	10	14.7	3	11.1	6	18	23	15.4
Dir. of social affairs	2	9.1	13	19.1	3	11.1	8	24	26	17.4
Dir. of training....	20	90.8	62	91.1	24	88.8	32	96	138	92.0
Ed. of publications.	6	27.2	25	36.8	9	33.3	15	45	55	36.7
Elem. school principal............	11	50.0	30	44.1	12	44.4	16	48	69	46.0
High school principal............	4	18.2	21	30.9	14	51.8	21	63	60	40.0
Librarian.........	20	90.8	68	100.0	27	100.0	33	100	148	98.7
Registrar.........	18	81.7	60	88.2	27	100.0	33	100	138	92.0
Supt. of buildings..	11	50.0	50	73.5	22	81.4	33	100	116	77.4
Vice-president.....	2	9.1	14	20.5	2	7.4	9	27	27	18.0
Average number of officers per institution.........	8.7		11.3		12.1		15.0		11.8	

This table should be read as follows: In 22 colleges enrolling under 300 students there are 3 or 13.6%, which have business managers.   In the 68 colleges enrolling 300–799 there are 27 or 39.7%, which have business managers, etc.

The chief storekeeper, the chief accountant, and the superintendent of buildings and grounds are frequently administratively responsible to the business agent. This practice is found

TABLE VII

AVERAGE TEACHING LOAD PER WEEK OF ADMINISTRATIVE OFFICERS IN 150 STATE TEACHERS COLLEGES. 1932

Titles of Administrative Officers	22 Colleges Enrollment Under 300		68 Colleges Enrollment 300–799		27 Colleges Enrollment 800–1199		33 Colleges Enrollment 1200 and Above		All Colleges Combined	
	Frequency	Av. No. Hours per Week	Frequency	Av. No. Hours per Week	Frequency	Av. No. Hours per Week	Frequency	Av. No. Hours per Week	Frequency	Av. No. Hours per Week
Business manager....	3	0	27	0	11	0	21	0	62	0
Bursar..............	4	0	17	0	10	0	11	0	42	0
Chief accountant.....	5	0	26	0	11	0	16	0	58	0
Chief storekeeper....	5	0	16	0	9	0	13	0	43	0
Dean of college......	7	7.5	35	5.0	16	6.0	22	4.3	80	5.2
Dean of men........	8	10.7	37	12.0	17	7.0	23	9.2	85	10.0
Dean of women......	18	6.0	54	5.4	25	4.0	30	2.5	127	4.5
Dir. of adjustment....	0	*	6	5.5	2	8.0	6	6.0	14	6.0
Dir. of athletics......	15	9.6	62	11.8	23	10.3	31	7.2	131	10.1
Dir. of extension.....	7	7.0	25	5.0	14	4.6	23	5.4	69	5.2
Dir. of health........	8	7.6	44	7.5	18	5.8	25	5.5	95	6.6
Dir. of housing......	4	10.0	12	9.8	7	10.0	6	0	29	7.8
Dir. of instruction....	3	12.0	5	10.2	3	9.0	6	5.2	17	8.5
Dir. of personnel.....	0	*	5	9.1	0	0	7	5.7	12	7.1
Dir. of placement....	7	12.0	33	7.5	14	8.0	27	1.7	81	6.0
Dir. of research......	0	*	12	10.2	4	12.0	11	9.0	27	10.0
Dir. of student activities..............	4	12.4	10	10.0	3	15.0	6	5.0	23	9.8
Dir. of social affairs..	2	12.0	13	8.7	3	7.0	8	3.0	26	7.0
Dir. of training......	20	5.0	62	6.3	24	6.0	32	4.5	138	5.6
Ed. of publications...	6	14.0	25	11.0	9	6.3	15	8.8	55	10.0
Elem. school principal	11	10.8	30	6.4	12	9.0	16	4.7	69	7.2
High school principal.	4	12.7	21	9.8	14	7.2	21	7.0	60	7.7
Librarian............	20	3.5	68	2.0	27	2.1	33	3.0	148	2.4
Registrar............	18	2.0	60	1.1	27	1.1	33	1.0	138	1.2
Supt. of buildings....	11	0	50	0	22	0	33	0	116	0
Vice-president.......	2	12.0	14	8.1	2	8.0	9	5.0	27	7.3

This table should be read as follows: In 22 colleges enrolling fewer than 300 students there are 3 business managers none of whom teaches, there are 7 college deans who teach an average of 7.5 hours per week, etc.

*No officials with this title in colleges under 300 enrollment. Hence there is no average teaching load.

TABLE VIII

<small>INTERRELATION OF THE BUSINESS AGENT AND OTHER ADMINISTRATIVE OFFICERS IN 150 TEACHERS COLLEGES. 1932</small>

$N = No.\ of\ Business\ Agents$

Items of Interrelation	22 Colleges Enrollment Under 300 $N = 7$	68 Colleges Enrollment 300–799 $N = 44$	27 Colleges Enrollment 800–1199 $N = 21$	33 Colleges Enrollment 1200 or Above $N = 32$	All Colleges Enrollment Combined $N = 104$
	Frequency	Frequency	Frequency	Frequency	Frequency
1. Instructional departments headed by the business agent					
A. None.........	7	44	21	32	104
2. Other offices held by the business agent					
A. None.........	5	30	12	20	67
B. Chief accountant..........	0	5	3	1	9
C. Chief storekeeper........	0	0	0	1	1
D. Purchasing agent.........	0	0	1	1	2
E. Registrar......	1	4	3	6	14
F. Secretary-treasurer......	1	3	0	2	6
G. Sup't. of buildings and grounds	0	2	2	1	5
3. Officers to whom the business agent is administratively responsible					
A. President......	7	43	21	32	103
B. Board of trustees...........	0	1	0	0	1
C. All others.....	0	0	0	0	0
4. Administrative officers responsible to the business agent					
A. Chief accountant..........	0	4	1	4	9
B. Chief storekeeper........	0	5	1	6	12
C. Sup't. of buildings and grounds	1	7	3	4	15
D. All others.....	1	1	1	1	4

This table should be read as follows: In colleges enrolling fewer than 300 students there are 7 business agents none of whom is a head of an instructional department, 5 hold no other office, 1 is registrar etc.

in thirty-six of the 150 institutions. In other words, presidents in thirty-six teachers colleges make subordinate business officers responsible to the business agent. In contrast to this practice business officers of all rank are directly responsible to the president in 114 teachers colleges.

It seems reasonable to assume that two or more business officers in the same institution who are directly responsible to the president will each tend to build a separate and independent unit rather than develop a special phase of a unified business department. Direct administrative responsibility for all business officers is contrary to Criterion 17, page 23, which states that administrative organization should provide for the grouping of related functions under the control of an officer who in turn is responsible to the president. The practice of making all business officers responsible to the business agent and the business agent directly responsible to the president is in harmony with the criterion as validated.

II. COLLEGE DEANS

More than half of the institutions in this study have a college dean in their administrative organization. Table VI, page 52, shows that the larger the college enrollment the greater the probability that there will be a dean. Approximately one-third of the small colleges have a dean. A dean is found in slightly more than one-half of the medium sized and large colleges. The extra large colleges employ a dean in two-thirds of the cases. The average teaching load of the dean grows less as the college enrollment grows larger. In the small colleges the teaching load of the dean is approximately eight hours per week, one-half of that recommended by the American Association of Teachers Colleges as a maximum load for full-time teachers. The medium sized and large colleges assign their deans approximately one-third of a teaching load. The extra large colleges recognize that greater enrollment increases the amount of time the dean must devote to administrative duty, by reducing his teaching load to an average of approximately four hours per week.

A summary of the data which show the interrelations between the college dean and other administrative officers appears in

Table IX.   In a majority of cases the dean is not head of an instructional department.   This relationship does not seem to be determined by the enrollment.   In colleges enrolling between 800 and 1199 students more than half of the deans are heads of instructional departments and yet this is not true of colleges in which the enrollment is larger nor is it true in medium sized colleges.   There are but seven of the twenty-two colleges with an enrollment under 300 which have a dean; however, four of the seven deans are heads of instructional departments.   These deans, who are also heads of instructional departments, are in a majority of cases from the department of education.   The department of mathematics has the next greatest frequency. Since educational administration is as a rule most frequently taught by the department of education, and since the dean's duties are administrative, those colleges which must group the deanship with the head of an instructional department meet the criterion that administrative organization should group related functions for performance by making the head of the department of education the college dean.

A further study of Table IX reveals the interrelation with respect to administrative responsibility.   All deans, regardless of the size of the colleges in which they work, are directly responsible to the president.   On the other hand, in only a small percentage of the cases involved are other officers administratively responsible to the dean.   The dean of men, the director of extension, the director of research, the director of training, the librarian, and the registrar are occasionally administratively responsible to the dean.   Such relationships are more frequently found in the larger colleges.   A further examination of Table IX reveals that thirty-two of the eighty deans included in this study hold other administrative offices.   These offices include those of the director of extension, director of instruction, director of placement, director of training, registrar, and vice-president.   The most frequent combination is that of dean and registrar.

An examination of the tables in Chapter VI indicates that functions performed by directors of instruction or vice-presidents in institutions having such officers are in other institutions performed by the college dean.   A careful study of the original data in this study shows that institutions having vice-

TABLE IX

INTERRELATIONS BETWEEN THE DEANS OF THE COLLEGES AND OTHER
ADMINISTRATIVE OFFICERS IN 150 TEACHERS COLLEGES. 1932
N = No. of Deans

Items of Interrelation	22 Colleges Enrollment Under 300 $N = 7$	68 Colleges Enrollment 300–799 $N = 35$	27 Colleges Enrollment 800–1199 $N = 16$	33 Colleges Enrollment 1200 or More $N = 22$	150 Colleges Enrollment Combined $N = 80$
	Frequency	Frequency	Frequency	Frequency	Frequency
1. Instructional departments headed by the college dean					
A. None.........	3	21	6	15	45
B. Education.....	3	8	5	2	18
C. Mathematics..	1	3	1	1	6
D. All others.....	0	3	4	4	11
2. Other offices held by the college dean					
A. None.........	1	22	11	14	48
B. Dir. of extension	2	1	0	1	4
C. Dir. of instruction..........	0	2	0	2	4
D. Dir. of placement.........	1	1	2	0	4
E. Dir. of training	0	2	0	0	2
F. Registrar......	2	5	2	1	10
G. Vice-president .	0	1	0	3	4
H. All others.....	1	1	1	1	4
3. Officers to whom the college dean is administratively responsible					
A. President......	7	35	16	22	80
B. All others.....	0	0	0	0	0
4. Administrative officers responsible to the college dean					
A. Director of athletics.........	1	2	1	1	5
B. Dir. of extension	0	0	0	4	4
C. Dir. of research	0	2	0	2	4
D. Dir. of training	0	1	2	2	5
E. Librarian......	0	2	1	2	5
F. Registrar......	0	4	0	2	6
G. All others.....	2	3	0	3	8

This table should be read as follows: In 22 colleges enrolling under 300 students there are 7 deans. Three of these deans are not heads of instruction departments; 1 holds no other office; 2 are directors of extension; 7 are administratively responsible to the president, etc.

presidents or directors of instruction seldom have a college dean. One officer frequently has two titles, such as vice-president and dean, or vice-president and director of instruction. All three of these officers are administratively responsible to the president, and since they perform similar functions it seems safe to assume that they are to a large extent holding similar positions under different titles.

III. DEANS OF MEN AND WOMEN

It may be observed by an examination of Table VI, page 52, that the institutions cooperating in this study have eighty-five deans of men serving in 56.7 per cent of the colleges. They are distributed in the small, medium sized, large, and extra large colleges with an increasing percentage from the smaller to the larger colleges. Table VII, page 53, shows their average teaching load varies from seven to twelve hours per week with the smallest average found in institutions enrolling 800 to 1199 students.

Some instructional departments are headed by deans of men. This occurs in thirty-one of the eighty-five institutions which include this officer in their organization. Table X shows that the heads of the departments of science and physical education are more frequently deans of men than are other department heads. Two comments made by presidents in reporting data for this investigation offer possible explanations for these combinations. "The head of our science department is dean of men. Not because he is head of the science department but because the classes in that department are small and the head has time to devote to administration." The comment regarding the combining the office of head of the physical education department with that of the dean of men is quite different. "The head of our department of physical education knows all of our men. He is in close contact with their activities. These acquaintanceships and these contacts led me to appoint him dean of men."

The office of dean of men is more frequently combined with that of the director of athletics than with any other office. Other offices combined with the dean of men include the director of extension, the director of placement, and the registrar. However, such combinations are quite limited and in a large majority of cases the office of dean of men is not combined with any other in the college. Deans of men are in all but one of the institutions investigated in this study administratively responsible to the president. No other officers are reported as responsible to the dean of men. This indicates that the func-

TABLE X

INTERRELATIONS BETWEEN THE DEANS OF MEN AND OTHER ADMINISTRATIVE OFFICERS IN 150 TEACHERS COLLEGES. 1932

N = No. of Deans of Men

Items of Interrelation	22 Colleges Enrollment Under 300 $N = 8$	68 Colleges Enrollment 300–799 $N = 37$	27 Colleges Enrollment 800–1199 $N = 17$	33 Colleges Enrollment 1200 or Above $N = 23$	150 Colleges Enrollment Combined $N = 85$
	Frequency	Frequency	Frequency	Frequency	Frequency
1. Instructional departments headed by deans of men					
A. None.........	4	22	12	14	54
B. Physical education..........	1	4	1	2	8
C. Practical arts..	0	1	0	1	2
D. Science.......	1	6	3	4	14
E. All others.....	2	2	1	2	7
2. Other offices held by deans of men					
A. None.........	6	28	12	17	63
B. Dir. of athletics	1	3	1	2	7
C. Dir. of extension	0	2	1	0	3
D. Dir. of placement.........	0	0	1	1	2
E. Registrar......	0	2	0	1	3
F. All others.....	1	2	2	2	7
3. Officers to whom the deans of men are administratively responsible					
A. President......	8	37	17	22	84
B. Dean of the college..........	0	0	0	1	1
4. Officers administratively responsible to the deans of men..	0	0	0	0	0

This table should be read as follows: In colleges enrolling fewer than 300 students there are 8 deans of men, 4 of whom are not heads of instructional departments, 1 dean of men is head of the physical education department, etc.

tions performed by the dean of men will probably be an independent unit of administration rather than a special aspect of a unified and integrated personnel program.

It is evident from Table VI, page 52, that the office of dean of women is well established in teachers colleges of all sizes. The office is found in 85 per cent of all the colleges included in this study. Although the large and extra large colleges more frequently include a dean of women in their administrative organization than do the medium sized and small colleges, the percentage of difference is small. In all colleges included in the study, the dean of women is administratively responsible to the president.

In Table XI it may be observed that the deans of women are generally not heads of instructional departments. This may indicate that the deans of women in the institutions reporting carry too heavy a load to serve as a department head in addition to the administrative duties of the dean of women's office. Further evidence supporting this assumption is indicated by the fact that ninety-seven deans of women hold no other offices in the colleges. The average teaching load of the deans of women varies from six hours per week in the small colleges to two and one-half hours per week in the extra large colleges. With the exception of the business officers who do not teach, the deans of women have the lightest teaching load of any of the administrative officers reported in this investigation. These facts indicate that deans of women are primarily engaged in non-classroom activities.

Some institutions combine the office of dean of women with health and housing activities. Seven directors of housing are administratively responsible to deans of women. In fourteen colleges the dean of women also carries the title of director of housing. An analysis of the performance of administrative functions which appears in Chapter V shows that deans of women often direct the functions pertaining to housing of students along with other duties. Five deans of women are heads of health departments. Four directors of health are administratively responsible to the dean of women. These facts indicate that some institutions are grouping these functions and thereby making the office of dean of women more inclusive.

TABLE XI

INTERRELATIONS BETWEEN THE DEANS OF WOMEN AND OTHER ADMINIS-
TRATIVE OFFICERS IN 150 TEACHERS COLLEGES. 1932
N = No. of Deans of Women

Items of Interrelation	22 Colleges Enrollment Under 300 N = 18	68 Colleges Enrollment 300–799 N = 54	27 Colleges Enrollment 800–1199 N = 25	33 Colleges Enrollment 1200 or Above N = 30	150 Colleges Enrollment Combined N = 127
	Frequency	Frequency	Frequency	Frequency	Frequency
1. Instructional departments headed by deans of women					
A. None	14	39	22	28	103
B. Home economics	0	4	0	1	5
C. Health	0	5	0	0	5
D. Languages	1	1	2	0	4
E. Social studies	1	2	1	0	4
F. All others	2	3	0	1	6
2. Other offices held by deans of women					
A. None	15	37	19	26	97
B. Director of housing	0	9	3	2	14
C. Director of social affairs	0	5	2	2	9
D. School nurse	1	1	1	0	3
E. All others	2	2	0	0	4
3. Officers to whom the deans of women are administratively responsible					
A. President	18	54	25	30	127
B. All others	0	0	0	0	0
4. Administrative officers responsible to the deans of women					
A. Director of health	1	2	1	0	4
B. Director of housing	1	2	2	2	7
C. All others	0	0	0	0	0

This table should be read as follows: In 22 colleges enrolling fewer than 300 students there are 18 deans of women; 14 of them are not heads of instructional departments, 1 is also head of a language department, etc.

In nine institutions the dean of women is also director of social affairs.   This is evidence that some college heads consider the direction of social affairs as consisting of duties different from those usually performed by the dean of women and yet so closely allied that the two offices are combined under the control of one individual.   On the other hand, Chapter V shows that many institutions delegate the management of social affairs to the dean of women as a regular part of her official duties.

IV. DIRECTORS OF ADJUSTMENT OR FOLLOW-UP SERVICE

An examination of Table VI, page 52, reveals that approximately 10 per cent of the colleges included in this study have appointed an official to follow the graduates of the institution into the field and help them in making their professional adjustments.   This officer is found more frequently in the larger institutions.   In fact, none of the small colleges reported such an officer.   In Table VII, page 53, it is revealed that the teaching load of these officials is, on the average, six hours per week.   This might indicate that a major share of their time and energy is devoted to adjustment service.   However, other interrelationships make this assumption doubtful.   Seven directors of training are also directors of adjustment service.   In four other institutions the director of adjustment is also responsible for the direction of placement service.   Since only fourteen institutions report such an officer, and since eleven of the fourteen hold some other office, in addition to an average teaching load of six hours per week, it is probably safe to assume that the interrelations of directors of adjustment service are such that only a limited portion of time and energy can be devoted to following the graduates into the field to help them with their problems of professional and personal adjustment to their new situations.

V. DIRECTORS OF ATHLETICS

In striking contrast to other administrative officers, the directors of athletics are in a large percentage of cases heads of instructional departments.   As would be expected, this department is that of physical education in nearly all cases.   Table XII shows that ninety-two of the 131 directors of athletics are department heads and that eighty-six of the ninety-two are heads of the department of physical education. Only in colleges enrolling fewer than 300 students are more than half of the directors not heads of departments. A possible explanation of

TABLE XII

INTERRELATIONS BETWEEN THE DIRECTOR OF ATHLETICS AND OTHER ADMINISTRATIVE OFFICERS IN 150 TEACHERS COLLEGES. 1932

N = No. of Directors of Athletics

Items of Interrelation	22 Colleges Enrollment Under 300 N = 15	68 Colleges Enrollment 300–799 N = 62	27 Colleges Enrollment 800–1199 N = 23	33 Colleges Enrollment 1200 or Above N = 31	150 Colleges Enrollment Combined N = 131
	Frequency	Frequency	Frequency	Frequency	Frequency
1. Instructional departments headed by directors of athletics					
A. None.........	8	18	4	9	39
B. Physical education..........	6	43	16	21	86
C. All others.....	1	1	3	1	6
2. Other offices held by the directors of athletics					
A. None.........	14	59	20	29	122
B. Dean of men...	1	3	1	2	7
C. All others.....	0	0	2	0	2
3. Officers to whom the directors of athletics are administratively responsible					
A. Dean of the college...........	1	2	1	1	5
B. Head department of physical education..	0	3	1	1	5
C. President......	14	57	21	29	121
D. All others.....	0	0	0	0	0
4. Officers administratively responsible to the directors of athletics.............	0	0	0	0	0

This table should be read as follows: In 22 colleges enrolling under 300 students there are 15 directors of athletics; 8 of them are not heads of instructional departments; 6 are heads of the department of physical education, etc.

this difference between small colleges and those enrolling a greater number of students is that some small colleges do not have departmental heads. Table VII, page 53, shows that the director of athletics teaches a heavier load on the average than any other administrative official. Probably this may be accounted for on the basis that athletic teaching is sometimes classified as laboratory instruction and a greater number of hours is required. All evidence reported in this study indicates that the directors of athletics, by being heads of the physical education departments and by teaching in the classroom, are more closely allied with the college instructional program than other officers of administration.

Table XII shows that some institutions combine the office of dean of men and director of athletics. This combination was noted in the discussion concerning deans of men. It was suggested in that discussion that one possible explanation for combining these offices in the few recorded cases is that the director of athletics probably knows more about the men in the college than any other staff member. This knowledge about the men on the campus would in all probability be valuable to the dean of men. A further examination of Table XII shows that 121 of the 131 directors in the colleges investigated are administratively responsible to the president. In five colleges the directors of athletics are responsible to the dean of the college and in five other institutions they are responsible to the head of the department of physical education. In none of the 131 colleges having a director of athletics were any cases reported where other officers were administratively responsible to the director of athletics.

VI. DIRECTORS OF EXTENSION

Table VI, page 52, shows that the office of director of extension is established in small, medium sized, large, and extra large teachers colleges. As colleges increase in size there is a greater percentage of them with directors of extension. In the extra large colleges this officer is found in two-thirds of the cases. In the small colleges there is not quite one in three which has a director of extension. In Table VII, page 53, it may be observed that the director of extension teaches a load of varying amounts in the different sized colleges. The teaching

TABLE XIII

INTERRELATIONS BETWEEN THE DIRECTOR OF EXTENSION AND OTHER
ADMINISTRATIVE OFFICERS IN 150 TEACHERS COLLEGES. 1932
N = No. of Directors of Extension

Items of Interrelation	22 Colleges Enrollment Under 300 $N = 7$ Frequency	68 Colleges Enrollment 300–799 $N = 25$ Frequency	27 Colleges Enrollment 800–1199 $N = 14$ Frequency	33 Colleges Enrollment 1200 or Above $N = 23$ Frequency	150 Colleges Enrollment Combined $N = 169$ Frequency
1. Instructional departments headed by directors of extension					
A. None.........	4	17	12	19	52
B. Education.....	1	4	0	2	7
C. Psychology....	1	1	1	0	3
D. All others.....	1	3	1	2	7
2. Other offices held by directors of extension					
A. None.........	4	11	13	14	41
B. Dean of college	2	1	0	1	4
C. Dean of men...	0	2	1	0	3
D. Director of placement.....	0	4	0	4	8
E. Director of publicity.........	0	1	0	0	1
F. Registrar......	0	3	1	1	5
G. All others.....	1	3	0	3	7
3. Officers to whom the directors of extension are administratively responsible					
A. Dean of college	0	0	0	4	4
B. President......	7	24	14	18	63
C. Registrar......	0	1	0	1	2
D. All others.....	0	0	0	0	0
4. Officers administratively responsible to the directors of extension					
A. Director of placement.....	0	0	0	2	1
B. All others.....	0	0	0	0	0

This table should be read as follows: In 22 colleges enrolling under 300 students there are 7 directors of extension; 4 of them are not heads of instructional departments; 1 is head of the department of education, etc.

load averages from seven hours per week in the small colleges to four and six-tenths hours per week in the large colleges. One would expect that the least teaching by directors of extension would occur in the extra large colleges. Those twenty-three directors in the extra large colleges teach more hours on the average each week than do the directors in the medium sized and large colleges. Table XIII shows that directors of extension in extra large colleges more frequently hold two administrative offices than do those in the large colleges. These facts indicate that size of enrollment does not determine the average teaching load of directors of extension. Neither does it determine whether or not the director of extension will also hold some other administrative office.

Several other facts appear in Table XIII. Only a few instructional departments are headed by directors of extension. That department most frequently headed by the director of extension is education. Extension in its nature means off-campus service or at least service to off-campus students. This is probably the reason why directors of extension are not heads of instructional departments. The one requires traveling, and the other, campus service. One might expect small colleges to combine the position of head of an instructional department with the director of extension more frequently than large or extra large institutions. The data from the limited number of small colleges having directors of extension prohibits any positive statement that a predominant practice exists. However, in the seven small institutions having directors of extension there are three who are heads of instructional departments. Eight directors of extension are also directors of placement. The knowledge which comes to the director of extension as he travels throughout the state should make him more valuable in placement service. The registrar is director of extension in five institutions. Since the registration of extension students and the recording of their grades are functions similar to those performed by the registrar on the campus, much can be said in favor of combining these two offices.

Administrative responsibility for directors of extension is highly centralized. Sixty-three of the sixty-nine directors of extension are administratively responsible to the president. In four large institutions the directors of extension are responsible to the dean.   Unless the president is constantly on guard, extension instruction under a director who is not responsible to the dean may develop into a separate institution with its own standards which may be different from those which control campus instruction.

VII. DIRECTORS OF HEALTH SERVICE

An examination of Table XIV shows that directors of health service are not dividing their time and energy between health and some other type of service.   Whenever a director of health service heads an instructional department, it is either health education or physical education.   Twenty-two health education departments are headed by directors of health service.   These twenty-two departments are well distributed in colleges of all sizes.   The thirteen departments of physical education headed by directors of health service are in the small and medium sized institutions.   Regardless of the size of the colleges, directors of health service hold no other offices in the institution included in this study.   Out of 150 colleges there is but one other office combined with health service and in but a single instance. This is the office of the dean of men.

Administrative relationships between directors of health service and other officers are highly centralized.   Eighty-six of ninety-five directors are administratively responsible to the president.   In just a few cases is the director of health service responsible to the dean of women.   A careful checking of the four institutions in which this relationship exists reveals that all four institutions have nurses as their directors of health service.   Several of the original reports from other institutions stated that the college nurse is administratively responsible to the dean of women.   This responsibility of the nurse to the dean of women was reported frequently enough to indicate that such a relationship is not mere chance.

Table VI, page 52, shows that approximately 64 per cent of all the institutions reporting have established a directorship of health service.   Small institutions are much less likely to have an established health service with a director, than larger ones. This is shown by the fact that the percentage of established health departments in small institutions is only slightly above

TABLE XIV

INTERRELATIONS BETWEEN THE DIRECTOR OF HEALTH SERVICE AND
OTHER ADMINISTRATIVE OFFICERS IN 150 TEACHERS COLLEGES. 1932
N = No. of Directors of Health Service

Items of Interrelation	22 Colleges Enrollment Under 300 $N = 8$	68 Colleges Enrollment 300–799 $N = 44$	27 Colleges Enrollment 800–1199 $N = 18$	33 Colleges Enrollment 1200 or Above $N = 25$	150 Colleges Enrollment Combined $N = 95$
	Frequency	Frequency	Frequency	Frequency	Frequency
1. Instructional departments headed by directors of health service					
A. None.........	3	28	12	17	60
B. Health education..........	4	4	6	8	22
C. Physical education..........	1	12	0	0	13
2. Other offices held by directors of health service					
A. None.........	8	43	18	25	94
B. Dean of men...	0	1	0	0	1
3. Officers to whom the directors of health are administratively responsible					
A. President......	7	39	17	23	86
B. Dean of women	1	2	1	0	4
C. All others.....	0	3	0	2	5
4. Officers administratively responsible to the directors of health service.....	0	0	0	0	0

This table should be read as follows: In 22 colleges enrolling under 300 students there are 8 directors of health service; 3 of them are not heads of instructional departments; 4 are heads of the health education departments, etc.

half that of the percentage of health departments in all the colleges combined.   Table VII, page 53, shows that on the average directors of health service teach nearly seven hours per week. The average number of hours taught per week in the different sized colleges does not vary greatly.   The range is from 7.6 hours in the small colleges to 5.5 hours in the extra large colleges.

Table XIV, page 68, refers to health service, health education, and physical education.   An examination of the catalogs of the institutions concerned shows that the terms are frequently used as synonymous.   In other institutions careful distinctions are made.   From catalog descriptions health service refers to medical, dental, nursing, and psychiatric services; health education refers to instruction in hygiene, nutrition, and physiology; physical education refers to play, games, gymnastics, and other forms of physical recreation.

VIII. DIRECTORS OF HOUSING

There is a total of twenty-nine directors of housing in the 150 teachers colleges included in this study.   This is approximately 20 per cent of the entire group.   Table VI, page 52, shows that they are well distributed in the colleges of various sizes, with the smallest percentage in those institutions enrolling 300 to 799 students.   Table VII, page 53, shows that directors of housing teach on the average one-half of the maximum load of sixteen hours per week.   This amount varies from twelve hours per week in the small colleges to a teaching load of zero hours in the extra large colleges.   Table XI, page 61, shows that fourteen directors of housing are also deans of women. The original data show that four others are nurses.   These data indicate that the functions of housing may be combined successfully with either the office of the dean of women or health service.   All directors of housing are administratively responsible to the president.

IX. DIRECTORS OF PERSONNEL

The office of the director of personnel is established in but twelve of the 150 teachers colleges.   Five of these directors are in medium sized and seven are in extra large institutions.   Their teaching load is slightly more than seven hours per week on the average.   Other offices held by directors of personnel include that of college dean, registrar, dean of men, director of placement, and alumni secretary.   All directors of personnel are administratively responsible to the president.

A check of the functions performed by directors of personnel shows little agreement concerning their relationship in the institutions employing such an officer. In the twelve institutions concerned there is agreement in only three of them regarding some of the functions which should be delegated to the director of personnel. These functions are (1) supervising the maintenance of scholarship standards, (2) keeping students' personnel records, and (3) providing a time schedule for courses to be offered. Some institutions use a director of personnel to do the work ordinarily done by a dean of women; others make personnel work almost exclusively placement service; still others make it mental hygiene. These data seem to indicate that teachers colleges are groping for a better way to handle their personnel problems, but as yet there is no clear-cut administrative organization which has won general adoption in the various colleges.

X. DIRECTORS OF PLACEMENT

Table VI, page 52, shows that more than half of the teachers colleges included in this study have placement service centralized under the control of a director. These directors teach an average of six hours per week. In the small teachers colleges the classroom load is twelve hours as compared with slightly less than two hours in the extra large colleges. This difference in teaching load is probably a recognition of the heavier placement responsibilities in larger institutions.

One of the outstanding facts revealed by Table XV is that the majority of placement directors hold other administrative positions. This may be due to the seasonal character of placement service. Combining placement with other administrative functions under the direction of one officer is found in institutions of all sizes. The most frequent combination is that of director of placement and director of training. This combination occurs in one-third of the institutions having a placement officer. The registrar, the dean, the director of extension, and director of adjustment service are officers who in different institutions also hold the position of director of placement. If placement is too seasonal in character to warrant a full-time officer, then any of the above combinations have merit. The director of training, because of his relations with students during the period of practice teaching, will secure valuable informa-

TABLE XV

INTERRELATIONS BETWEEN THE DIRECTOR OF PLACEMENT AND OTHER
ADMINISTRATIVE OFFICERS IN 150 TEACHERS COLLEGES. 1932
N = No. of Directors of Placement

Items of Interrelation	22 Colleges Enrollment Under 300 $N = 7$	68 Colleges Enrollment 300–799 $N = 33$	27 Colleges Enrollment 800–1199 $N = 14$	33 Colleges Enrollment 1200 or Above $N = 27$	150 Colleges Enrollment Combined $N = 81$
	Frequency	Frequency	Frequency	Frequency	Frequency
1. Instructional departments headed by directors of placement					
A. None	5	26	9	23	63
B. Education	1	6	5	3	15
C. Psychology	1	1	0	0	2
D. All others	0	0	0	1	1
2. Other offices held by directors of placement					
A. None	5	9	1	11	26
B. Dean of college	1	1	2	0	4
C. Dir. adjustment	0	2	0	2	4
D. Dir. extension	0	4	0	4	8
E. Dir. training	1	13	7	6	27
F. Registrar	0	4	0	0	4
G. All others	0	0	2	2	4
3. Officers to whom the directors of placement are administratively responsible					
A. President	7	33	14	25	79
B. Director of extension	0	0	0	1	1
C. Dir. training	0	0	0	1	1
4. Officers administratively responsible to the directors of placement	0	0	0	0	0

This table should be read as follows: In 22 colleges enrolling under 300 students there are 7 directors of placement; 5 of them are not heads of instructional departments; 1 is head of the department of education, etc.

tion which will contribute to his efficiency as director of placement.   Both the dean and the registrar will know the students
well by the time they graduate.   Since a knowledge of the
ability of the student to be recommended is essential in placement service, either the dean or the registrar, by the nature of
his other duties, would be partially prepared to handle placement.   Another essential in placement is knowledge concerning
the schools and communities to which graduates are being recommended.   The director of extension, by his off-campus contacts, learns to know these schools and communities.   Placement and adjustment service each contributes to the other.
The officer who recommends a graduate for a specific position
is naturally interested in helping that individual make his professional adjustments.   These combinations are in accord with
the criterion which states that related functions should be
grouped under the direction or control of an administrative
officer who in turn is responsible to the president.

Practically all directors of placement are administratively
responsible to the president with no other officers responsible to
them.   The fact that 33 per cent of the directors of placement
are also directors of training indicates a close relationship between these officers.   However, the relationship is not such that
full-time placement officers are made administratively responsible to the director of training.

XI. DIRECTORS OF RESEARCH

Table VI, page 52, shows that approximately one teachers
college in five has an officer designated as director of research.
Since it is quite generally conceded that the appointment of a
special director of research in teachers colleges is a new venture,
a report that 20 per cent of the institutions have such an officer
would indicate that special administrative provision is being
made for research.   However, other data reveal that this
provision is very limited in scope.   Table VII, page 53, shows
that directors of research teach an average of ten hours per week.
This means that better than 60 per cent of the time of the directors of research is devoted to teaching.   There is additional
evidence that other relationships reduce the time devoted to
research.   Fourteen of the twenty-seven directors of research

are heads of instructional departments. In addition, three directors of research hold other administrative positions; one is director of extension, another directs placement, a third is dean of the college. These facts indicate that directors of research are not given much free time to carry forward research projects.

XII. DIRECTORS OF STUDENT ACTIVITIES

Table VI, page 52, shows that approximately one institution in six has an officer with this title. These officers are well distributed throughout the colleges with various enrollments. Their teaching load, as indicated in Table VII, page 53, varies from twelve hours in the small colleges to five hours in the extra large ones. The average teaching load is approximately ten hours per week. In several colleges this office is combined with some other office such as that held by the college dean, the director of placement, the dean of men, or the dean of women. In all cases this officer is reported as directly responsible to the president.

Several comments concerning the direction of student activities were made by those furnishing data for this study. Fourteen presidents stated that the student council under the leadership of a faculty adviser functioned in the direction of student activities. Other comments were, "a part of the dean of women's work," "handled by a committee," "a graduate manager functions in this capacity."

The small percentage of institutions having such an officer, the combination of those offices with others, and comments such as those quoted above seem to indicate that the consensus of opinion is that there is little felt need for such an officer in teachers colleges.

XIII. DIRECTORS OF STUDENT SOCIAL AFFAIRS

Table VI, page 52, shows twenty-six officers with this title. It is evident from a check of the original data that this officer is in nearly all cases doing the same work as that of the dean of women. In nine of the twenty-six cases they have both titles; that is, they are listed as dean of women and director of social affairs. In all cases they are administratively responsible to the president.

In those institutions having directors of social affairs they are, as a rule, made responsible for helping formulate policies concerning student social activities, planning social activities, supervising general conduct at social affairs, keeping the calendar of social events, and granting permits to use college buildings for social affairs. However, these functions are, in the majority of institutions, performed by the dean of women when delegated to a single administrative officer. The chief difference between deans of women and directors of social affairs is that deans of women manage social affairs and in addition perform other functions, such as housing and student welfare. Chapter V presents data which bear out the above statements and warrant the conclusion that the dean of women as an administrative officer usually is responsible for functions ordinarily performed by the director of social affairs.

XIV. DIRECTORS OF TRAINING

It may be observed in Table VI, page 52, that 92 per cent of the colleges reporting in this study have a director of training. Regardless of size, the percentage of institutions having this office established is high. It is desirable to know how institutions which have no director of training take care of functions usually delegated to this office. To answer this question a careful examination was made of the reports from the twelve institutions not having this office. In a majority of cases it was found that two or three people supervised student-teaching with no one individual in charge of all of the work. In other words, a high school principal might have charge of student-teaching in the secondary school, and an elementary principal might have a similar responsibility for those college students whose practice teaching was done in an elementary grade. Since the two principals were independent of each other, no director of training was listed.

Teaching by the director of training is a common practice in the institutions studied. For all of the colleges combined, the director of training teaches on the average 5.6 hours per week. This is slightly more than one-third of the regular teaching load. One would expect a greater teaching load for directors of training in the small colleges. This is not the case. Directors in medium sized and large colleges teach on the average more hours than those in small institutions.

Several facts appear in Table XVI. Directors of training are frequently heads of departments of education. This predominant practice may represent an effort to combine theory and practice in education for the purpose of integrating the two phases of the subject. Another predominant practice is to combine the placement office with the directorship of the training school. This occurs in twenty-seven colleges, with the percentage of frequency increasing as the college enrollment becomes larger.

The office of the director of adjustment or follow-up service is a part of the training school office in seven institutions. Since only fourteen colleges reported a director of adjustment service, these seven cases show a predominant practice toward administering adjustment service as a continuation of practice teaching. Practically all directors of training are administratively responsible to the president. In four institutions heads of departments of education are those to whom directors of training are administratively responsible. In five other institutions directors of training are responsible to the dean. Two officers are frequently responsible to the director of training. These are the elementary school principal and the high school principal. Thirty-five elementary principals out of a total of sixty-nine, and fifty-two high school principals out of a total of sixty are administratively responsible to the director of training.

XV. EDITORS OF PUBLICATIONS

In Table VI, page 52, it may be seen that fifty-five colleges of the 150 included in this study have an editor of publications. They teach an average of ten hours per week. Table VII, page 53, shows that the amount of teaching decreases as the size of the institution increases. Twelve of the fifty-five editors are heads of English departments. This indicates that some presidents make publications a departmental responsibility. It is probably safe to assume that the head of the English department is as well qualified as any other member of the staff to serve as editor of publications. In all cases the editors of publications are administratively responsible to the president. The editors of college publications work in cooperation with deans, presi-

TABLE XVI

INTERRELATIONS BETWEEN THE DIRECTOR OF TRAINING AND OTHER ADMINISTRATIVE OFFICERS IN 150 TEACHERS COLLEGES. 1932

N = No. of Directors of Training

Items of Interrelation	22 Colleges Enrollment Under 300 N = 20	68 Colleges Enrollment 300–799 N = 62	27 Colleges Enrollment 800–1199 N = 24	33 Colleges Enrollment 1200 or Above N = 32	150 Colleges Enrollment Combined N = 138
	Frequency	Frequency	Frequency	Frequency	Frequency
1. Instructional departments headed by directors of training					
A. None.........	13	48	17	22	100
B. Education.....	6	14	7	10	37
C. All others.....	1	0	0	0	1
2. Other offices held by directors of training					
A. None.........	18	40	14	24	96
B. Dean of college	0	2	0	0	2
C. Dir. of adjustment.........	0	5	2	0	7
D. Dir. of placement..........	1	13	7	6	27
E. All others.....	1	2	1	2	6
3. Officers to whom directors of training are administratively responsible					
A. Dean of college	0	1	2	2	5
B. Head of education department	0	2	0	2	4
C. President......	20	59	22	28	129
4. Officers administratively responsible to director of training					
A. Elem. principal	2	13	8	12	35
B. H. S. principal.	4	13	8	17	52
C. All others.....	0	0	1	2	3

This table should be read as follows: In 22 colleges enrolling under 300 students there are 20 directors of training. Thirteen of them are not heads of any instructional departments; 6 of them are heads of departments of education, etc.

dents, and committees in formulating policies concerning publicity and publications, in maintaining informational service, in editing and publishing institutional bulletins, and in distributing information concerning campus and extension courses. One might expect the editor of publications to have chief responsibility in directing the preparation of the catalog. However, the dean or president more frequently has the responsibility of the preparation of the college catalog. This probably indicates that presidents consider the preparation of the catalog a function which cannot be successfully delegated.

XVI. LIBRARIANS

A glance at Table VI, page 52, shows that all but two of the 150 colleges included in this study have librarians in their administrative organizations. These two institutions are among the small group of colleges. Correspondence with their administrative heads revealed that one institution managed its library through a committee with the registrar at its head. The other had developed a cooperative plan with a near-by city library by which it was stated splendid service was obtained. The librarian teaches an average of 2.4 hours per week. This amount is approximately the same for institutions of all sizes. Table XVII shows that twenty-five of the 148 librarians are heads of library science departments. In nearly all cases the librarians hold no other administrative offices. Two librarians edit the college publications; two others serve as college registrars. In five cases the librarian is administratively responsible to the dean of the college. In all other cases the responsibility is directly to the president. In no instances are officers outside of the library staff directly responsible to the librarian for administrative leadership.

XVII. REGISTRARS

The registrar is found more frequently in the administrative organizations of teachers colleges than any other officers except the president, the librarian, and the director of training. Table VI, page 52, shows that 92 per cent of the colleges have a registrar. Table VII, page 53, shows that he teaches on the

average a little more than one hour per week.   That there is no
predominant practice toward making the registrar head of any

TABLE XVII

Items of Interrelation	22 Colleges Enrollment Under 300 *N = 20*	68 Colleges Enrollment 300–799 *N = 68*	27 Colleges Enrollment 800–1199 *N = 27*	33 Colleges Enrollment 1200 or Above *N = 33*	150 Colleges Enrollment Combined *N = 148*
	Frequency	Frequency	Frequency	Frequency	Frequency
1. Instructional departments headed by librarians					
A. None.........	19	60	17	24	120
B. Library science	0	7	9	9	25
C. All others.....	1	1	1	0	3
2. Other offices held by the librarians					
A. None.........	17	65	27	32	141
B. Ed. of publications..........	0	2	0	0	2
C. Registrar......	2	0	0	0	2
D. All others.....	1	1	0	1	3
3. Officers to whom the librarian is administratively responsible					
A. Dean of college	0	2	1	2	5
B. President......	20	66	26	31	143
4. Officers administratively responsible to the librarian......	0	0	0	0	0

This table should be read as follows: In 22 colleges with enrollment under 300 there are 20
librarians.   Nineteen of these librarians are not heads of instructional departments; 17 of
them hold no other offices, etc.

instructional department is shown in Table XVIII.   On the
other hand, many registrars hold a second office.   Fourteen of
them serve as business agents for the colleges.   Ten others are
college deans as well as registrars.   In all, about one registrar
in three holds two administrative positions.

One might expect to find registrars in small colleges holding
two offices more frequently than in large ones.   However, the

percentage of combinations is about the same regardless of the size of the institutions concerned. The most frequent combination, that with the business agent, is difficult to justify. As was pointed out in Chapter II, the business agent's functions

TABLE XVIII

INTERRELATIONS BETWEEN THE REGISTRAR AND OTHER ADMINISTRATIVE OFFICERS IN 150 TEACHERS COLLEGES. 1932

$N = No.$ of Registrars

Items of Interrelation	22 Colleges Enrollment Under 300 $N = 18$	68 Colleges Enrollment 300–799 $N = 60$	27 Colleges Enrollment 800–1199 $N = 27$	33 Colleges Enrollment 1200 or Above $N = 33$	150 Colleges Enrollment Combined $N = 138$
	Frequency	Frequency	Frequency	Frequency	Frequency
1. Instructional departments headed by the registrar					
A. None	16	59	26	33	134
B. Education	1	0	1	0	2
C. All others	1	1	0	0	2
2. Other offices held by the registrar					
A. None	13	40	19	22	94
B. Business agent	1	4	3	6	14
C. Dean of college	2	5	2	1	10
D. Dean of men	0	2	0	1	3
E. Dir. of extension	0	3	1	1	5
F. Dir. of placement	0	4	0	0	4
G. All others	2	2	2	2	8
3. Officers to whom the registrar is administratively responsible					
A. Dean	0	4	0	2	6
B. President	18	56	27	31	132
4. Officers administratively responsible to the registrar					
A. Dir. of extension	0	1	0	1	2
B. All others	0	0	0	0	0

This table should be read as follows: In 22 colleges enrolling under 300 students there are 18 registrars. Sixteen of them are not heads of instructional departments; 13 of them hold no other administrative offices, etc.

are quite different from those of the registrar.   Ability to perform the functions of one office is not the same as that required
to perform the functions of the other.   In other words, the
purchasing of supplies and the classification of students are so
different that it is difficult to see how either can help in the performance of the other.   On the other hand, any knowledge
which the registrar has concerning the graduates could be
utilized in recommending students for positions.   This is probably the basis for making the registrar director of placement.

The administrative responsibility of the registrar is well centralized.   In all but six institutions the registrar is directly
responsible to the president.   When not responsible to the
president, he is responsible to the dean of the college. In only
two institutions are other administrative officers responsible
to the registrar.   In both cases the officer so responsible is the
director of extension.   In some other institutions different
officers are administratively responsible to registrars who have
their office combined with that of college dean or business agent.
Such responsibility is not indicated in Table XVIII because it
is apparently due to the other office in the combination that the
responsibility is so delegated.   For example, a librarian responsible to a college dean who is also registrar is in all probability responsible to this officer because he is dean, and not because
he is registrar.

XVIII. SUPERINTENDENTS OF BUILDINGS AND GROUNDS

Table VI, page 52, shows that 77 per cent of the colleges included in this study have a superintendent of buildings and
grounds.   Every one of the extra large institutions includes
this officer in its organization.   As the enrollment in colleges
grows smaller the percentage having a superintendent of buildings and grounds grows less.   In institutions not having this
officer, the usual arrangement reported was a foreman in each
building who went directly to the president for instruction and
supervision.   One institution reported that a committee chairman directed the buildings and grounds staff.

The superintendent of buildings and grounds seldom teaches.
No average teaching load was computed because of the over-
whelming percentage of institutions which reported no teaching

for these officers. In this respect the superintendent of buildings and grounds is classified with the business manager, the
bursar, the chief accountant, and the chief storekeeper, who
are likewise non-teaching officers. Five institutions reported
heads of instructional departments serving as superintendents of
buildings and grounds. Three of these were heads of the manual training department. It seems safe to assume that any
individual well qualified in manual training would have much
knowledge and many skills which would prove valuable in
superintending the upkeep and maintenance of college buildings
and grounds.

Several other facts appear in Table XIX. The office of
business agent is in five institutions combined with the office of
superintendent of buildings and grounds. Such a combination
meets the criterion that related functions should be grouped for
administrative control and performance. All superintendents
of buildings and grounds not responsible to the president of
their respective institutions are responsible to the business
agent. In none of the 116 institutions which reported a superintendent of buildings and grounds were other administrative
officers apart from the buildings and grounds staff administratively responsible to this officer.

XIX. TRAINING SCHOOL PRINCIPALS

An examination of Table VI, page 52, shows that there are
sixty-nine elementary school principals and sixty high school
principals in the colleges included in this study. The greatest
percentage of elementary school principals is found in schools
enrolling under 300 students, while the colleges enrolling 1200
or more students have the highest percentage of high school
principals. Table VII, page 53, shows that, all institutions
considered, the high school principal carries a heavier teaching
load than the elementary principal. The teaching load of each
decreases as the colleges increase in enrollment.

Training school principals are administratively responsible
to the president or to the director of training. Thirty-four
elementary principals and eight principals of high schools are
responsible directly to the president. Since 92 per cent of all
the institutions included in the study have directors of training,

it means that a large percentage of them does not have administrative control over the elementary school, and a limited number does not have administrative control over the high school.

TABLE XIX

INTERRELATIONS BETWEEN THE SUPERINTENDENT OF BUILDINGS AND GROUNDS AND OTHER ADMINISTRATIVE OFFICERS IN 150 TEACHERS COLLEGES. 1932

N = No. of Superintendents of Buildings and Grounds

Items of Interrelation	22 Colleges Enrollment Under 300 $N = 11$	68 Colleges Enrollment 300–799 $N = 50$	27 Colleges Enrollment 800–1199 $N = 22$	33 Colleges Enrollment 1200 or Above $N = 33$	150 Colleges Enrollment Combined $N = 116$
	Frequency	Frequency	Frequency	Frequency	Frequency
1. Instructional departments headed by the superintendent of buildings and grounds					
A. None.........	11	48	20	32	111
B. Man. training..	0	2	1	0	3
C. Mathematics..	0	0	1	0	1
D. Chemistry.....	0	0	0	1	1
2. Other offices held by superintendents of buildings and grounds					
A. None.........	10	47	19	31	107
B. Business agent.	0	2	2	1	5
C. All others.....	1	1	1	1	4
3. Officers to whom the superintendents of buildings and grounds are administratively responsible					
A. Business agent.	1	7	3	4	15
B. President......	10	43	19	29	101
4. Officers administratively responsible to the superintendents of buildings and grounds.........	0	0	0	0	0

This table should be read as follows: In 22 colleges enrolling under 300 students there are 11 superintendents of buildings and grounds. None of them is a head of an instructional department; 10 of them hold no other office, etc.

Such administrative relationships are in opposition to the criterion that administrative organization should provide for the grouping of related functions under the direction or control of an officer who, in turn, is responsible to the president. It seems reasonable to assume that a director of training without administrative jurisdiction in either elementary or secondary schools would be handicapped in building an integrated program of student-teaching.

SUMMARY

1. Twenty-six different administrative officers are found in 5 per cent or more of the various internal administrative organizations of the 150 teachers colleges included in this investigation.

2. The following officers are established in more than 50 per cent of the colleges investigated: business agent, dean of college, dean of men, dean of women, director of athletics, director of health, director of placement, director of training, librarian, registrar, and superintendent of buildings and grounds.

3. Officers established in less than 25 per cent of the colleges are: director of adjustment, director of housing, director of instruction, director of personnel, director of research, director of student activities, director of social affairs, and vice-president.

4. Those officers who usually carry the heaviest teaching load are: dean of men, director of athletics, director of instruction, director of research, director of student activities, and editor of publications.

5. Business agents, superintendents of buildings and grounds, and registrars usually are non-teaching officers.

6. The business agent in a majority of cases holds no other office. He is responsible to the president. There is a predominant practice of making the chief storekeeper, the chief accountant, and the superintendent of buildings and grounds administratively responsible to the business agent.

7. The college dean, if head of a department at all, will probably be head of the education department. In nearly half of the cases he holds two offices. All deans are administratively responsible to the president.

8. Deans of men are not generally heads of instructional departments. A few institutions combine the office with that of

director of athletics.   Practically all deans of men are administratively responsible to the president of the institution.

9. Deans of women are generally not heads of instructional departments.   The offices which are combined with that of the dean of women most frequently concern health and housing activities.   The dean of women is responsible to the president.

10. There are only a few institutions with an officer charged with the responsibility of directing adjustment service.   These officers are usually directors of training or of placement.

11. The director of athletics is usually head of the department of physical or health education.   He seldom holds two administrative offices.   In nearly all cases he is responsible to the president.   No other officers are responsible to him.

12. A few directors of extension are heads of departments of education or psychology.   However, in nearly all cases this officer heads no instructional department.   About one-third of the directors of extension hold some other office.   Administrative responsibility is in nearly all cases to the president.   Practically no other officers are responsible to directors of extension.

13. Directors of health service are frequently heads of departments of health or physical education.   There is no predominant practice for directors of health service to hold other offices.   Nearly all directors of health are administratively responsible to the president.   No other officers are responsible to the directors of health.

14. Directors of housing are frequently deans of women or college nurses.   They are administratively responsible to the president.

15. Only a few colleges have directors of personnel.   Their functions are not alike in different colleges.   Administrative responsibility is to the president.

16. Directors of placement are in a few cases heads of the departments of education.   A frequent practice is to combine this office with the directorship of the training school.   Directors of placement are administratively responsible to the president.   No other officers are responsible to them.

17. Directors of research are established in but few colleges. They are often heads of instructional departments or hold other offices.   They are directly responsible to the president.

18. Directors of student activities usually hold some other

office, such as dean of men or dean of women. They are not department heads. Their administrative responsibility is to the president.

19. The office of the director of student social affairs is frequently held by the dean of women. Those officials having this title perform about the same functions as deans of women.

20. Directors of training are found in 92 per cent of the colleges investigated. About one-third of them are heads of education departments. They are frequently assigned to perform the functions of the director of placement. They are practically all administratively responsible to the president. The principals of the elementary and high schools are in the majority of cases responsible to the directors of training.

21. The office of librarian is well established in institutions of all sizes. A large percentage of colleges have departments of library science with the librarian as head. Few librarians hold other offices. In nearly all cases the librarian is administratively responsible to the president. No officers other than members of the library staff are responsible to the librarian.

22. The registrar is very seldom head of an instructional department. Some teachers colleges combine the office of registrar with that of business agent or dean. The registrar is responsible to the president. No other officials are administratively responsible to the registrar.

23. Superintendents of buildings and grounds are noninstructional officers. Sometimes the office is combined with that of the business agent. In some institutions the superintendent of buildings and grounds is administratively responsible to the business agent; however, in a large majority of the cases responsibility is to the president.

24. Training school principals are only occasionally heads of departments. They are administratively responsible to the president or to the director of training. They direct a staff, but no other officers are responsible to them.

CRITICAL EVALUATION

Those administrative officials who teach in addition to their administrative duties are forced to keep up in two fields. Except in cases where classroom instruction will contribute to administrative efficiency, this condition is in opposition to the criterion which favors specialization of administrative officers. If administrative duties which are similar can be grouped under the direction or control of one officer, a greater degree of specialization is possible and fewer administrative officers will be necessary.

Standards for the American Association of Teachers Colleges recommend sixteen hours per week in classroom instruction as the maximum load. Several institutions reported a full teaching load for their administrative officers. Institutions of approximately the same number of students assign administrative officers to teach amounts varying from two to sixteen hours. Heavy teaching assignments for administrative officers are not in accord with the criterion which states that administrative organization should provide opportunity for the instructional staff to teach in their various departments without being overburdened with administrative duties. Institutions assigning heavy teaching loads along with administrative duties are in danger of causing their officers to neglect both instruction and administration. Those institutions which assign practically a full teaching load in addition to administrative duties are expecting double performance from administrative officers. Such double duty could probably be avoided by alternating courses, increasing the number assigned to different classes, and grouping related functions for administrative control.

The data in this chapter do not indicate any predominant practice for combining administrative functions and having full-time administrative officers. On the contrary, the practice of giving a heavy teaching load to several officers is prevalent. As a rule, each of these officers is administratively responsible to the president. Not only does such an arrangement prevent specialization in administration, but the president, by increasing the number of administrative officers, thereby increases the multiplicity of his duties in directing and controlling these officers. The number of interviews will increase. A constant vigilance must be maintained to prevent duplication and omissions. The amount of office space will necessarily be enlarged and the clerical staff will either be increased or the time of its members parceled out to various officers. Our validated criteria which give high ratings to specialization in administration and the freeing of the president from a multiplicity of routine duties, indicate that many institutions could improve their internal organization by reducing the total number of officers, freeing them from responsibility for teaching in the classroom, and grouping closely related functions under the control of one officer with assistants when necessary. Such an arrangement would free the members of the instructional staff and give them more time for the improvement of their courses, for personal conferences with students, and for research.

CHAPTER V

THE PERFORMANCE OF ADMINISTRATIVE FUNCTIONS

ANY administrative organization in teachers colleges has for its purpose the furtherance of the performance of functions necessary in carrying forward the activities of the institution. The titles of administrative officers used in the various institutions with their interrelations concerning administrative responsibility and combinations of offices held give one picture of internal organization. Another picture just as important for an understanding and an evaluation of internal administrative organization is a summary of the performance of functions by the various officers included within the different institutions. Such a summary is presented by tables and discussion in this chapter.

The purpose in presenting this material is to show predominant practices and differences in the performance of functions in teachers colleges of various sizes and to make possible an evaluation, in the light of administrative criteria, of the internal organization as expressed through functional performance. The following specific questions will be answered:

1. What functions do presidents usually retain for their own management and direction?
2. What functions are usually performed by subordinate officers?
3. What subordinate officers usually have the responsibility for the performance and control of the various related groups of administrative functions?
4. When functions are performed by two or more administrative officers, what ones usually share in having responsibility for performance?
5. What functions are usually performed by groups?
6. Which representative functions are frequently not performed?

7. How does performance of functions as found in practice agree with criteria validated by a jury of teachers college presidents who were designated by their colleagues as superior administrators?

These questions will be answered in tables and discussions concerning each related group of administrative functions. Finally, a summary and critical evaluation will be given.

INTERPRETING THE DATA CONCERNING FUNCTIONAL
PERFORMANCE

The percentages recorded in the tables in this chapter do not in any case represent 100 per cent of the ways in which functions were reported as being performed in the various institutions. Lack of space in the tables prohibited the recording of all the different officers and groups by whom the administrative functions are performed. Available space in the tables permitted the recording of only such practices as are common to several institutions. One function when performed by two or more officers or groups increases the percentages recorded for both of them. The data are intended to show the percentage of institutions in which a particular officer, such as the dean, the registrar, or the director of training, performs the function under consideration or shares in the performance of the function. *The data are not intended to show 100 per cent of the ways in which officers share responsibility for performance of functions.* A reference to Table XX will clarify this point. The president is listed as sharing responsibility for formulating policies concerning admission, registration, and records of students in 41.4 per cent of all colleges investigated. Since this function is shared with other officials, such as the dean or the registrar, these latter officials will be recorded as sharing the same responsibility.

The data are recorded in percentages in order to make comparison between groups of institutions possible. Since in the groups of the small, large, and extra large colleges one institution is equivalent to approximately 4 per cent of the group, agreement among a few institutions will make relatively large percentages. In reading the tables in this chapter it is necessary to keep in mind that not all the colleges investigated perform all the functions under consideration.

TABLE XX

ADMISSION, REGISTRATION, CLASSIFICATION, AND RECORDS OF STUDENTS

THE PERFORMANCE OF ADMINISTRATIVE FUNCTIONS IN 22 SMALL, 68 MEDIUM SIZED, 27 LARGE, AND 33 EXTRA LARGE TEACHERS COLLEGES. 1932

Functions and Chief Administrative Officers and Groups Who Usually Perform Them	Percentage of Colleges in Which One Officer or Group Usually Performs the Administrative Function					Percentage of Colleges in Which Two or More Officers or Groups Usually Cooperate in Performing the Function				
	Enrollment					Enrollment				
	Under 300	300 to 799	800 to 1199	1200 or More	All Colleges Combined	Under 300	300 to 799	800 to 1199	1200 or More	All Colleges Combined
1. Formulating policies concerning admission, registration, and students' records										
A. Dean of the college..............	0	4.4	3.0	0	2.8	18.2	27.9	40.7	30	29.4
B. Faculty as a whole	0	0	0	3	.7	22.7	5.9	7.4	24	12.8
C. President........	9.1	4.4	3.7	0	4.1	59.0	55.9	40.7	30	41.4
D. Registrar.......	0	4.4	3.7	18	6.7	45.4	38.2	51.8	42	36.1
E. State board.....	22.7	5.9	3.7	0	6.7	9.1	11.8	18.5	0	10.0
2. Approving policies concerning admission, registration, and records										
A. Dean of college..	0	4.4	0	3	2.8	13.6	14.7	25.9	15	16.7
B. Faculty as a whole	9.1	4.4	3.7	15	7.4	13.6	5.9	0	27	10.7
C. President.......	22.7	19.1	18.5	12	18.1	31.8	45.6	33.3	51	42.8
D. Registrar.......	0	1.5	0	6	2.0	9.1	26.5	29.6	12	21.4
E. Standing committee................	4.5	2.9	7.4	0	3.4	4.5	11.8	7.4	3	8.1
F. State board.....	31.8	7.5	7.4	3	10.0	9.1	16.7	48.1	6	18.7
3. Evaluating high school credits										
A. Dean of college..	4.5	10.3	11.1	6	8.7	13.6	8.8	14.8	12	11.4
B. President.......	13.6	1.5	0	0	2.8	13.6	11.8	7.4	3	9.4
C. Registrar.......	41.0	41.2	48.1	57	46.1	77.2	8.8	37.0	30	26.1
D. Standing committee................	13.6	2.9	7.4	0	4.8	0	10.3	7.4	15	9.4
4. Evaluating credits from other colleges										
A. Dean of college..	13.6	13.2	14.8	9	12.8	18.2	8.8	14.8	18	13.4
B. President.......	22.7	4.4	0	0	5.4	9.1	16.7	3.7	6	10.7
C. Registrar.......	27.2	29.4	37.0	45	34.1	31.8	23.5	25.9	39	29.4
D. Standing committee................	13.6	7.5	11.1	0	6.1	0	10.3	11.1	18	10.7
5. Keeping students' academic records										
A. Dean of college..	0	5.9	0	0	2.8	4.5	0	14.8	3	4.1
B. Executive secretary................	9.1	0	3.7	0	2.0	0	2.9	0	0	1.4
C. Registrar.......	81.7	72.0	74.0	93	77.4	18.2	2.9	14.8	6	8.1
6. Classifying students										
A. Dean of college..	4.5	11.8	11.1	3	8.7	18.2	5.9	22.2	21	14.1
B. President.......	18.2	0	0	0	2.8	9.1	16.7	0	0	8.7
C. Registrar.......	31.8	36.8	25.9	48	36.7	22.7	22.1	18.5	36	24.8
D. Standing committee................	0	5.9	8.8	0	6.7	0	4.4	14.8	15	8.1

TABLE XX—(*Continued*)

Functions and Chief Administrative Officers and Groups Who Usually Perform Them	Percentage of Colleges in Which One Officer or Group Usually Performs the Administrative Function					Percentage of Colleges in Which Two or More Officers or Groups Usually Cooperate in Performing the Function				
	Enrollment					Enrollment				
	Under 300	300 to 799	800 to 1199	1200 or More	All Colleges Combined	Under 300	300 to 799	800 to 1199	1200 or More	All Colleges Combined
7. Keeping students' personnel records										
A. Dean of college..	0	2.9	3.7	3	2.8	9.1	2.9	14.8	18	9.4
B. Dean of men....	0	0	0	3	.7	18.2	11.8	22.2	33	20.7
C. Dean of women..	13.6	7.5	3.7	3	6.7	27.2	14.7	25.9	33	18.7
D. Director of personnel............	0	2.9	0	12	3.4	0	0	0	12	2.8
E. Registrar.......	50.0	38.2	29.6	18	34.1	27.2	19.1	7.4	57	20.0
8. Checking requirements for certificates, diplomas, and degrees										
A. Dean of college..	4.5	11.8	3.7	3	7.4	9.1	4.4	25.9	27	14.1
B. President.......	13.6	1.5	0	0	2.8	18.2	8.8	0	0	6.7
C. Registrar.......	41.0	54.4	44.4	54	49.4	18.2	16.7	25.9	27	20.7
D. Standing committee................	22.7	1.5	11.1	3	6.7	0	4.4	0	0	4.1
9. Supplying transcripts of records										
A. Dean of college..	0	7.5	0	0	3.4	0	2.9	7.4	3	3.4
B. Executive secretary...............	9.1	2.9	3.7	0	3.4	0	0	0	0	0
C. President.......	0	0	0	0	0	9.1	1.5	0	0	2.0
D. Registrar.......	95.3	73.5	81.4	93	82.0	9.1	29.0	7.4	3	4.8
10. Providing certificates, diplomas, and degrees										
A. Dean of college..	0	4.4	3.7	0	2.8	9.1	4.4	14.8	6	7.4
B. President.......	31.8	7.5	7.4	6	10.7	13.6	13.2	11.1	12	12.8
C. Registrar.......	31.8	30.9	37.0	54	37.4	18.2	14.7	14.8	9	14.1
D. State board.....	22.7	14.7	3.7	3	11.4	0	4.4	0	6	3.4
11. Awarding scholarships										
A. Faculty as a whole	13.6	2.9	3.7	0	4.1	4.5	1.5	0	0	1.4
B. President.......	22.7	19.1	18.5	12	18.1	13.6	14.7	3.7	15	12.8
C. Standing committee................	18.2	7.5	29.6	9	13.4	9.1	5.9	0	0	6.1
12. Guiding students in selection of courses										
A. Dean of college..	9.1	7.5	7.4	6	7.4	13.6	13.2	33.3	21	18.7
B. Dean of men....	0	0	0	0	0	4.5	14.7	11.1	0	9.4
C. Dean of women..	0	0	0	0	0	9.1	17.6	14.8	3	12.8
D. Faculty as a whole	4.5	4.4	3.7	0	2.8	9.1	7.5	11.1	9	8.7
E. Head of department..............	4.5	2.9	0	12	4.8	9.1	10.3	18.5	9	11.4
F. President.......	18.2	0	0	0	2.8	27.2	17.0	14.8	6	16.1
G. Registrar.......	9.1	1.5	0	0	2.0	4.5	22.1	18.5	33	21.4

This table should be read as follows: Full responsibility for formulating policies concerning admission, registration, records, and classification of students is delegated to the dean by none of the colleges enrolling fewer than 300; by 4.4% of the colleges enrolling 300–799; by 3% of the colleges enrolling 800–1199; and by none of the colleges enrolling more than 1200 students. In cooperation with other officials this responsibility is delegated to the dean by 18.2% of the colleges enrolling under 300, etc. Consult page 89 for a statement concerning the interpretation of data in this table.

ADMISSION, REGISTRATION, CLASSIFICATION, AND RECORDS OF
STUDENTS

Those administrative functions dealing with admission,
registration, classification, and records of students are performed to a large extent by three officials—the dean, the registrar, and the president.   An analysis of Table XX, page 90,
shows that the registrar, more than any other single official,
performs these functions with two exceptions.   The approval
of policies is in many institutions reserved to the president or
is a power of the state board.   In guiding students in the selection of courses, the registrar does not stand out as the one
official most frequently carrying this responsibility.   Here the
dean of the college, the heads of departments, and the president
have a large share of the responsibility.

The size of the institutions determines in some instances what
officer or agency shall perform a certain function.   As far as this
group of functions is concerned, the state boards restrict their
participation to the formulation and approval of policies and the
providing of certificates, diplomas, and degrees.   In all three
of these functions the state board retains the responsibility in a
greater percentage of cases in the smaller institutions.   It is
apparent from the data in Table XX that the state boards
usually perform fewer functions as institutions grow larger.   A
similar statement may be made concerning the president.   The
smaller the institution, the more likely that the president will
perform the function under consideration.   This is illustrated
in the performance of functions regarding evaluation of credits.
Nearly one-fourth of the presidents in small colleges evaluate
credits of students transferring from other colleges.   In the
larger institutions none of the presidents holds himself responsible for the performance of this function.

Some functions are predominantly performed by individuals
and others by groups.   Evaluating credits, keeping records,
classifying students, checking requirements for certificates,
supplying transcripts, and providing diplomas are functions
which in more than half of the institutions are performed by
individuals.   The formulation of policies, the approval of
policies, and the guidance of students in the selection of courses
are functions performed by groups or by two or more adminis-

trative officers.   The groups may be listed as the faculty as a whole and as committees of the faculty.   Formulation of policies, approval of policies, and awarding scholarships are functions performed by the faculty either as a single responsibility or as a cooperative responsibility along with administrative officers.   Standing committees are used to approve policies, to evaluate credits, and to classify students.   The data in Table XX show that several presidents use the faculty for making group judgments.   Committees, on the other hand, in the institutions where they are used, administer functions which in a greater number of colleges are delegated to individuals for performance.

BUILDINGS AND GROUNDS MANAGEMENT

A study of Table XXI, page 94, shows that in the main the president, the business manager, and the superintendent of buildings and grounds have responsibility for those functions necessary in carrying forward a program of buildings and grounds management.   The state board in the case of some institutions retains certain functions, but with the exception of supervising the erection of new buildings and approving recommendations for new equipment, the state boards, to a large measure, delegate to institutional officers other functions.   Heads of departments in some few institutions recommend new equipment.   In all other functions the heads of departments are reported as having no responsibility.

In eight of the sixteen functions reported, the president is the officer who usually performs the duties involved.   He formulates and approves policies concerning buildings and grounds. New buildings are in a large percentage of cases planned by the president, either alone or in cooperation with the state board. Repairs and alterations are directed by him, and he recommends and approves wage scales for buildings and grounds men.   New equipment is recommended by the president in three institutions out of ten, and in practically half of the institutions new equipment is approved by him.

In only a few institutions is the business agent responsible for functions dealing with buildings and grounds management. On the whole these are the institutions in which the office of the

TABLE XXI

BUILDINGS AND GROUNDS MANAGEMENT

THE PERFORMANCE OF ADMINISTRATIVE FUNCTIONS IN 22 SMALL, 68 MEDIUM SIZED, 27 LARGE, AND 33 EXTRA LARGE TEACHERS COLLEGES. 1932

Functions and Chief Administrative Officers and Groups Who Usually Perform Them	Percentage of Colleges in Which One Officer or Group Usually Performs the Administrative Function					Percentage of Colleges in Which Two or More Officers or Groups Usually Cooperate in Performing the Function				
	Enrollment					Enrollment				
	Under 300	300 to 799	800 to 1199	1200 or More	All Colleges Combined	Under 300	300 to 799	800 to 1199	1200 or More	All Colleges Combined
1. Formulating policies concerning buildings and grounds management										
A. Business agent...	9.1	11.8	7.4	3	8.7	9.1	23.5	14.8	24	20.0
B. Dean of college..	4.5	7.5	3.7	3	5.4	4.5	13.2	3.7	6	8.7
C. President.......	36.3	23.5	25.9	12	23.4	41.0	52.9	51.8	54	51.4
D. Superintendent of buildings and grounds	4.5	4.4	7.4	9	4.8	36.3	41.2	40.7	36	39.4
E. State board.....	4.5	2.9	3.7	3	2.8	4.5	2.9	7.4	6	4.1
2. Approving policies concerning buildings and grounds										
A. Business agent...	9.1	1.5	3.7	3	3.4	0	11.8	11.1	9	9.4
B. President.......	54.5	45.6	48.1	51	48.7	27.2	29.4	25.9	36	30.0
C. Superintendent of buildings and grounds	0	2.9	3.7	3	2.0	13.6	16.7	14.8	12	14.8
D. State board.....	9.1	7.5	7.4	6	7.4	13.6	5.9	7.4	3	6.7
3. Planning new buildings										
A. President.......	31.8	26.5	40.7	36	32.0	59.0	45.6	44.4	45	47.4
B. Special committee	4.5	2.9	11.1	3	4.1	13.6	4.4	7.4	12	8.1
C. Superintendent of buildings...........	0	2.9	3.7	6	2.8	13.6	7.5	18.5	12	11.4
D. State board.....	4.5	8.8	3.7	6	6.7	36.3	26.5	18.5	21	25.4
4. Planning repairs and alterations										
A. Business agent...	9.1	11.8	3.7	3	8.1	4.5	4.4	14.8	24	9.4
B. President.......	41.0	26.5	40.7	18	36.1	50.0	47.0	44.4	51	48.1
C. Special committee	0	0	0	0	0	0	0	0	3	0
D. Superintendent of buildings...........	9.1	8.8	3.7	15	9.4	31.8	26.5	14.8	36	27.4
5. Directing the making of repairs and alterations										
A. Business agent...	9.1	8.8	7.4	3	7.4	0	7.5	11.1	18	9.4
B. President.......	36.3	10.3	14.8	9	14.8	18.2	23.5	25.9	24	23.4
C. Superintendent of buildings...........	36.3	33.8	40.7	39	36.7	9.1	20.6	25.9	24	20.7
D. State board.....	0	5.9	7.4	3	4.8	9.1	5.9	11.1	6	7.4

TABLE XXI—(*Continued*)

Functions and Chief Administrative Officers and Groups Who Usually Perform Them	Percentage of Colleges in Which One Officer or Group Usually Performs the Administrative Function					Percentage of Colleges in Which Two or More Officers or Groups Usually Cooperate in Performing the Function				
	Enrollment					Enrollment				
	Under 300	300 to 799	800 to 1199	1200 or More	All Colleges Combined	Under 300	300 to 799	800 to 1199	1200 or More	All Colleges Combined
6. Maintaining heat, light, and ventilation										
A. Business agent...	4.5	5.9	3.7	6	5.4	4.5	8.8	14.8	9	9.4
B. President.......	18.2	4.4	0	3	5.4	9.1	5.9	0	12	6.7
C. Superintendent of buildings..........	63.6	61.7	74.0	51	61.4	0	11.8	14.8	15	11.4
7. Maintaining sanitary conditions										
A. Business agent...	9.1	4.4	3.7	6	4.1	4.5	4.4	18.5	3	6.7
B. Director of health service.............	4.5	7.5	7.4	3	6.1	9.1	8.8	3.7	6	7.4
C. President.......	18.2	4.4	0	3	5.4	13.6	5.9	0	12	7.4
D. Superintendent of buildings and grounds	54.5	48.5	59.2	54	52.8	9.1	16.7	25.9	12	16.1
8. Planning the campus landscaping										
A. Business agent...	4.5	1.5	3.7	3	2.8	4.5	4.4	14.8	6	6.7
B. President.......	36.3	16.7	18.5	3	16.7	41.0	39.7	44.4	42	41.4
C. Special committee	4.5	2.9	14.8	6	6.1	4.5	4.4	3.7	18	7.4
D. Superintendent of grounds............	27.2	29.4	25.9	24	27.4	31.8	32.3	29.6	36	32.8
E. State board.....	4.5	2.9	7.4	6	4.1	4.5	8.8	7.4	9	8.1
9. Keeping lawns, flowers, and shrubs in condition										
A. Business agent...	4.5	2.9	3.7	6	4.1	4.5	8.8	7.4	3	6.7
B. President.......	9.1	7.5	7.4	3	6.7	22.7	5.9	3.7	6	8.1
C. Standing committee................	0	0	11.1	6	3.2	4.5	5.9	3.7	9	6.1
D. Superintendent of grounds............	59.0	64.7	62.9	69	64.8	22.7	13.2	11.1	9	13.4
10. Managing the maintenance staff										
A. Business agent...	9.1	2.9	11.1	18	8.1	4.5	2.9	3.7	3	3.4
B. President.......	45.4	14.7	22.2	3	18.1	22.7	10.3	3.7	12	11.4
C. Superintendent of buildings and grounds	27.2	41.2	55.5	51	44.1	18.2	14.7	3.7	6	11.4
11. Directing the in-service-training of the maintenance staff										
A. Business agent...	4.5	4.4	7.4	18	8.1	4.5	2.9	3.7	3	3.4
B. President.......	31.8	11.8	7.4	3	12.0	13.6	7.5	11.1	9	9.4
C. Superintendent of buildings and grounds	13.6	38.2	22.2	39	32.0	18.2	7.5	3.7	9	8.7

TABLE XXI—(*Continued*)

Functions and Chief Administrative Officers and Groups Who Usually Perform Them	Percentage of Colleges in Which One Officer or Group Usually Performs the Administrative Function					Percentage of Colleges in Which Two or More Officers or Groups Usually Cooperate in Performing the Function				
	Enrollment					Enrollment				
	Under 300	300 to 799	800 to 1199	1200 or More	All Colleges Combined	Under 300	300 to 799	800 to 1199	1200 or More	All Colleges Combined
12. Recommending wage scales for various members of the buildings and grounds staff										
A. Business agent...	4.5	7.5	3.7	9	6.7	4.5	5.9	3.7	15	7.4
B. President.......	54.5	33.8	37.0	18	34.1	18.2	13.2	11.1	27	16.7
C. Superintendent of buildings and grounds	13.6	5.9	22.2	30	15.4	13.6	2.9	7.4	6	6.1
13. Approving wage scales for buildings and grounds staff										
A. Business agent...	4.5	1.5	3.7	3	2.8	4.5	7.5	7.4	6	6.7
B. President.......	50.0	48.5	66.6	60	54.8	50.0	11.8	7.4	24	19.4
C. State board.....	22.7	19.1	14.8	6	16.1	18.2	1.5	9.0	15	6.7
14. Supervising the erection of new buildings										
A. Business agent..	4.5	1.5	3.7	6	4.5	4.5	8.8	11.1	6	8.1
B. President........	22.7	16.7	25.9	6	16.7	36.3	20.6	29.6	36	28.1
C. Superintendent of buildings...........	9.1	10.3	18.5	15	12.8	18.2	5.9	18.5	6	10.0
D. State board.....	9.1	27.9	25.9	30	25.4	31.8	11.8	3.7	21	15.4
15. Recommending new equipment										
A. Business agent...	4.5	1.5	3.7	3	2.8	9.1	8.8	11.1	12	10.0
B. Head of department..............	0	5.9	11.1	18	8.7	13.6	7.5	18.5	24	14.1
C. President.......	41.0	30.9	40.7	9	29.4	45.4	30.9	29.6	39	34.8
D. Special committee	4.5	1.5	7.4	6	4.1	4.5	4.4	11.1	15	6.7
E. Superintendent of buildings...........	0	1.5	7.4	3	2.8	18.2	4.4	14.8	18	11.4
F. State board.....	0	5.9	7.4	3	4.8	13.6	5.9	7.4	15	9.4
16. Approving recommendations for new equipment										
A. Business agent...	0	0	0	3	.7	0	8.8	11.1	12	9.4
B. Head of department..............	4.5	0	0	3	1.4	4.5	2.9	0	9	4.1
C. President.......	41.0	33.8	62.9	39	41.4	22.7	23.5	14.8	45	26.7
D. State board.....	22.7	19.1	11.1	6	15.4	18.2	7.5	0	36	14.1

This table should be read as follows: Full responsibility for formulating policies concerning buildings and grounds management is delegated to the business agent by 9.1% of the colleges enrolling fewer than 300 students; by 11.8% of the colleges enrolling 300–799; by 7.4% of the colleges enrolling 800–1199; and by 3% of the colleges enrolling 1200 or more students. In cooperation with other officers this responsibility is delegated to the business agent by 9.1% of the colleges enrolling under 300, etc.
Consult page 89 for a statement concerning interpretation of data in this table.

business agent and the superintendent of buildings and grounds are combined under the direction of one person.   The superintendent of buildings and grounds is naturally an important officer in this field.   He helps the president in formulating policies.   He cooperates in planning new buildings and in making repairs and alterations.   He maintains light, heat, and ventilation, and is chiefly responsible for the maintenance of sanitary conditions.   Individually or in cooperation with other officials, he is responsible for planning the landscaping in more than half of the institutions, and then his staff keeps the lawn, flowers, and shrubs in condition.   He manages the maintenance staff and directs the in-service training of its members. In short, it is he who accepts the responsibility for keeping the plant in shape for carrying forward the activities of the college.

There are a few innovations listed in Table XXI which merit special comment.   The director of health service is, in 6 per cent of the colleges, responsible for maintaining sanitary conditions.   This seems to be putting special talent to work in maintaining conditions which will prevent illness.   One would expect that an even greater percentage of health officers would be used in the performance of this function in teachers colleges. In some institutions the presidents report that they themselves manage the maintenance staff, maintain heat, light, and ventilation; and in some institutions they report that they keep the lawns, flowers, and shrubs in condition.   Correspondence with those institutions reveals that the president serves as superintendent of buildings and grounds.   Such service may be necessary under financial conditions which are limited or curtailed. However, the performance of such duties by the president is not in accord with the criterion which states that the president should be relieved of a multiplicity of duties which may occupy his time to such an extent that major attention cannot be given to the development of administrative and institutional policies.

BUSINESS MANAGEMENT

Business management is almost entirely kept in the hands of the president with a business agent to carry out the necessary procedures.   Table XXII shows that other college officials,

TABLE XXII

BUSINESS MANAGEMENT

THE PERFORMANCE OF ADMINISTRATIVE FUNCTIONS IN 22 SMALL, 68 MEDIUM SIZED, 27 LARGE, AND 33 EXTRA LARGE TEACHERS COLLEGES. 1932

Functions and Chief Administrative Officers and Groups Who Usually Perform Them	Percentage of Colleges in Which One Officer or Group Usually Performs the Administrative Function					Percentage of Colleges in Which Two or More Officers or Groups Usually Cooperate in Performing the Function				
	Enrollment					Enrollment				
	Under 300	300 to 799	800 to 1199	1200 or More	All Colleges Combined	Under 300	300 to 799	800 to 1199	1200 or More	All Colleges Combined
1. Formulating policies concerning business management										
A. Business agent...	4.5	19.1	22.2	12	16.1	13.6	25.0	29.6	48	29.4
B. President.......	18.2	19.1	22.2	18	19.4	63.6	42.6	44.4	63	50.7
C. State board.....	13.6	5.9	3.7	3	7.4	27.2	19.1	8.5	12	18.7
2. Approving policies concerning business management										
A. Business agent...	9.1	7.5	3.7	6	6.7	4.5	20.6	11.1	12	14.8
B. President.......	45.4	32.3	66.6	51	44.8	18.2	32.3	11.1	30	26.1
C. State board.....	31.8	14.7	14.8	6	15.4	13.6	13.2	7.4	18	13.4
3. Estimating departmental needs										
A. Business agent...	13.6	7.5	3.7	0	6.1	4.5	23.5	14.8	30	20.7
B. Head of department..............	18.2	32.3	51.8	42	36.1	4.5	13.2	22.2	30	17.4
C. President.......	27.2	14.7	11.1	3	13.4	45.4	33.8	22.2	27	32.0
D. State board.....	4.5	1.5	0	3	2.0	18.2	7.5	0	3	6.7
4. Approving or denying departmental budget estimates										
A. Business agent...	9.1	1.5	3.7	0	2.8	4.5	17.6	18.5	18	16.1
B. President.......	50.0	52.9	66.6	51	54.8	27.2	26.5	29.6	33	28.7
C. State board.....	18.2	13.2	0	6	10.0	18.2	7.5	11.1	6	9.4
5. Consolidating departmental budgets into a budget for the college										
A. Business agent...	13.6	19.1	11.1	6	14.1	9.1	26.5	48.1	15	25.4
B. President.......	45.4	32.3	40.7	51	40.0	22.7	33.8	48.1	33	34.8
C. State board.....	4.5	1.5	0	3	2.0	4.5	8.8	3.7	6	6.7
6. Presenting the college budget for board approval or rejection										
A. Business agent...	4.5	1.5	0	6	2.8	4.5	7.5	7.4	3	5.4
B. President.......	59.0	79.4	92.5	78	78.1	4.5	10.3	7.4	6	8.1

TABLE XXII—(*Continued*)

Functions and Chief Administrative Officers and Groups Who Usually Perform Them	Percentage of Colleges in Which One Officer or Group Usually Performs the Administrative Function					Percentage of Colleges in Which Two or More Officers or Groups Usually Cooperate in Performing the Function				
	Enrollment					Enrollment				
	Under 300	300 to 799	800 to 1199	1200 or More	All Colleges Combined	Under 300	300 to 799	800 to 1199	1200 or More	All Colleges Combined
7. Requisitioning departmental supplies										
A. Business agent...	18.2	19.1	11.1	27	19.4	9.1	14.7	14.8	15	14.1
B. Head of department..............	27.2	38.2	70.3	45	44.1	4.5	7.5	3.7	12	7.4
C. President.......	22.7	10.3	3.7	3	9.4	27.2	17.6	3.7	9	14.8
8. Approving departmental requisitions										
A. Business agent...	9.1	8.8	11.1	24	12.8	13.6	20.6	18.5	15	18.1
B. President.......	50.0	47.0	55.5	39	47.4	22.7	27.9	22.2	21	24.8
C. State board.....	13.6	2.9	0	0	3.4	9.1	4.4	3.7	0	4.1
9. Keeping purchases for various departments within the budget as approved										
A. Business agent...	27.2	29.4	40.7	42	34.1	18.2	27.9	29.6	36	28.7
B. President.......	27.2	20.6	25.9	6	19.4	31.8	26.5	25.9	33	28.7
C. Executive secretary..............	4.5	5.9	0	0	3.4	9.1	1.5	0	0	2.0
10. Purchasing supplies										
A. Business agent...	31.8	51.5	66.6	60	53.4	9.1	11.8	22.2	12	13.4
B. President.......	41.0	7.5	11.1	3	12.0	9.1	10.3	11.1	6	9.4
C. State board.....	4.5	11.8	3.7	9	8.7	9.1	2.9	3.7	0	3.4
11. Storing and delivering supplies										
A. Business agent...	36.3	47.0	37.0	39	42.0	4.5	17.6	22.2	21	17.4
B. Superintendent of buildings and grounds	22.7	17.6	29.6	21	21.4	22.7	7.5	11.1	9	10.7
C. State board.....	9.1	2.9	0	3	3.4	9.1	1.5	0	3	2.8
12. Keeping financial records										
A. Business agent...	50.0	77.9	88.8	69	74.1	4.5	5.9	7.4	30	11.4
B. Registrar.......	27.2	1.5	0	9	6.7	13.6	1.5	0	3	3.4
C. State board.....	13.6	7.5	0	3	6.1	4.5	1.5	0	3	2.0
13. Preparing financial reports										
A. Business agent...	45.4	47.0	70.3	60	54.1	13.6	23.5	33.3	45	28.7
B. President.......	18.2	5.9	3.7	3	6.7	13.6	20.6	14.8	12	38.1
C. State board.....	13.6	5.9	0	0	4.8	4.5	2.9	0	0	2.0
14. Property accounting										
A. Business agent...	36.3	50.0	70.3	51	52.0	13.6	17.6	18.5	42	22.8
B. President.......	31.8	7.5	7.4	3	10.0	13.6	14.7	3.7	3	10.0
C. State board.....	9.1	1.5	0	0	2.0	4.5	1.5	0	0	1.4

TABLE XXII—(*Continued*)

Functions and Chief Administrative Officers and Groups Who Usually Perform Them	Percentage of Colleges in Which One Officer or Group Usually Performs the Administrative Function					Percentage of Colleges in Which Two or More Officers or Groups Usually Cooperate in Performing the Function				
	Enrollment					Enrollment				
	Under 300	300 to 799	800 to 1199	1200 or More	All Colleges Combined	Under 300	300 to 799	800 to 1199	1200 or More	All Colleges Combined
15. Managing payroll procedures										
A. Business agent...	36.3	54.4	66.6	60	55.4	18.2	17.6	22.2	21	20.0
B. President.......	18.2	7.5	11.1	15	11.4	22.7	17.6	14.8	6	15.4
C. State board.....	13.6	5.9	0	3	5.4	13.6	2.9	0	3	4.1
16. Insuring buildings										
A. Business agent...	18.2	23.5	22.2	24	22.8	9.1	17.6	14.8	18	16.1
B. President.......	22.7	1.5	18.5	3	8.1	18.2	17.6	7.4	12	14.8
C. State board.....	27.2	20.6	14.8	15	19.4	9.1	7.5	0	3	5.4
17. Providing summaries of cost records for various departmental services										
A. Business agent...	31.8	52.9	59.2	51	50.1	9.1	13.2	11.1	39	18.1
B. President.......	4.5	5.9	7.4	3	4.8	4.5	4.4	3.7	6	4.8
C. Registrar.......	22.7	0	0	9	5.4	4.5	0	0	3	1.4
D. State board.....	13.6	8.8	0	3	6.7	4.5	1.5	0	3	2.0
18. Requiring independent auditing of financial records										
A. Business agent...	9.1	13.2	18.5	18	14.8	4.5	2.9	7.4	9	5.4
B. President.......	36.3	8.8	11.1	27	17.4	4.5	4.4	0	3	2.8
C. State board.....	27.2	47.0	40.7	27	38.7	4.5	1.5	0	3	2.0
19. Disposing of salvaged material										
A. Business agent...	18.2	36.8	29.6	45	34.8	4.5	16.7	14.8	21	15.4
B. President.......	22.7	10.3	7.4	6	10.7	22.7	13.2	7.4	15	14.1
C. Superintendent of buildings and grounds	19.1	11.8	29.6	12	14.8	13.6	1.5	7.4	9	6.1
D. State board.....	18.2	8.8	7.4	6	9.4	4.5	4.4	3.7	3	4.1

This table should be read as follows: Full responsibility for formulating policies concerning business management is delegated to the business agent by 4.5% of the colleges enrolling fewer than 300 students; by 19.1% of the colleges enrolling 300–799; by 22.2% of the colleges enrolling 800–1199; and by 12% of the colleges enrolling 1200 or more students.   In cooperation with other officers this responsibility is delegated to the business agent by 13.6% of the colleges enrolling under 300, etc.
Consult page 89 for a statement concerning interpretation of data in this table.

such as the dean and the director of training, do not participate to any extent in business management.

The president retains chief responsibility in six of the nineteen business functions reported. He formulates and approves policies with the help of the business agent in approximately three institutions out of four. He approves or denies departmental estimates. He presents the college budget to the board for approval or rejection. Departmental requisitions must be approved by him. In about half of the institutions the president retains full or partial responsibility for keeping departmental purchases within the budget.

The business agent usually purchases the supplies. He helps the president keep these purchases within the budget. More than any other official he is responsible for storing and delivering supplies. The keeping of financial records is his responsibility. He prepares financial reports and accounts for property. In 75 per cent of the institutions he manages the payroll procedures. He insures the buildings, provides summaries of cost records, and disposes of salvaged material. In the majority of functions concerning accounting, finance, or property the business agent is the one official most likely to have the responsibility in the 150 teachers colleges investigated.

Some few business functions are in the main the responsibility of neither the president nor the business agent. Heads of departments usually estimate departmental needs and make departmental requisitions. In one institution out of three the superintendent of buildings and grounds has some responsibilities for storage and delivering supplies. He also has in many institutions responsibility for disposing of salvaged material.

The almost complete delegation of business functions by the state boards of control grows more nearly complete as the institutions increase in size. In some small institutions state boards retain functions of:

1. Formulating policies concerning business management.
2. Approving policies.
3. Approving or denying departmental budgets.
4. Consolidating departmental budgets into a budget for the college.
5. Approving departmental requisitions.

6. Purchasing, storing, and delivering supplies.
7. Keeping financial records.
8. Insuring buildings.

Although state boards in a few institutions retain business functions, on the whole they have delegated the responsibility more frequently than they have retained it.

CAMPUS INSTRUCTION

Many educators will concede that classroom instruction is the hub around which other college activities revolve. The delegation of those administrative functions pertaining to instruction is therefore fundamental in determining the strength and morale of the institution. It is evident from Table XXIII page 104, that the presidents of the 150 colleges included in this investigation delegate these functions to several different officers or groups for performance. However, it is clear that the presidents retain a large share in controlling and directing classroom instruction. In ten of the twenty-five major functions reported, the president, in larger percentages than other officers, is responsible for their direction and performance. These functions are:

1. Approving policies concerning campus instruction.
2. Approving new courses.
3. Assigning classrooms to instructors.
4. Assigning faculty members to teach various approved courses.
5. Formulating policies concerning campus instruction.
6. Keeping the teaching and extra-curricular load balanced for the instructional staff.
7. Planning commencement programs.
8. Providing for substitution in case of faculty absence.
9. Supervising the instruction of the probationary members of the staff.
10. Supervising the coordination of the various instructional departments.

An analysis of these ten functions shows that the presidents usually retain those functions of instruction which cause them to work with faculty members rather than with students. In addition to these primary functions, presidents frequently hold themselves responsible with one or two other officers for the direction and control of the following activities:

1. Determining required courses for various certificates and degrees.
2. Planning facilities for student teaching.
3. Supervising the maintenance of scholarship standards.

In addition, the data show many institutions with presidents performing or cooperating in the performance of other functions which for the majority of institutions investigated are delegated to a subordinate officer.

In several institutions the college dean is charged with the performance of functions which on the whole presidents usually retain as their own responsibility.   In other words, those functions usually retained by the presidents are, if delegated, usually assigned to the dean.   A specific illustration may be taken from Table XXIII.   The presidents in 24.8 per cent of the institutions assign classrooms to instructors.   As nearly as large a group of presidents delegate this function to their deans.   In the larger institutions this responsibility is more frequently delegated than retained.   Regardless of the size of the institution some responsibilities are usually delegated to the college dean. These functions are:

1. Providing a time schedule of courses˜to be offered.
2. Providing a schedule for final examinations.
3. Supervising the maintenance of scholarship standards.

The department heads usually have the responsibility for certain functions.   In the large and extra large institutions the responsibility for assigning faculty members to teach various approved courses is delegated to the head of the department. The head of the department, more than any other officer, helps the librarian in selecting books.   He is the president's chief assistant in supervising instruction of probationary members of the staff.   He is responsible more frequently than any other officer for:

1. Recommending courses to be offered by the department.
2. Recommending requirements for departmental majors and minors.
3. Recommending a time schedule for departmental courses.

TABLE XXIII

CAMPUS INSTRUCTION

THE PERFORMANCE OF ADMINISTRATIVE FUNCTIONS IN 22 SMALL, 68 MEDIUM SIZED, 27 LARGE, AND 33 EXTRA LARGE TEACHERS COLLEGES. 1932

Functions and Chief Administrative Officers and Groups Who Usually Perform Them	Percentage of Colleges in Which One Officer or Group Usually Performs the Administrative Function					Percentage of Colleges in Which Two or More Officers or Groups Usually Cooperate in Performing the Function				
	Enrollment					Enrollment				
	Under 300	300 to 799	800 to 1199	1200 or More	All Colleges Combined	Under 300	300 to 799	800 to 1199	1200 or More	All Colleges Combined
1. Approving policies concerning campus instruction										
A. Dean of college	0	5.9	7.4	6	5.4	9.1	10.3	22.2	36	18.1
B. Director of instruction..........	0	1.5	0	0	.7	4.5	4.4	3.7	9	5.4
C. Faculty as a whole	9.1	1.5	3.7	6	4.1	13.6	7.5	14.8	6	9.4
D. President.......	50.0	75.6	29.6	24	38.7	36.3	32.3	44.4	42	37.4
E. Stand. committee	4.5	5.9	7.4	0	4.8	4.5	7.5	7.4	12	8.1
F. State board.....	4.5	0	3.7	3	2.0	4.5	5.9	3.7	3	4.8
2. Approving new courses										
A. Dean of college	4.5	1.5	11.1	0	3.4	13.6	4.4	22.2	27	14.1
B. Director of instruction..........	0	1.5	3.7	0	1.4	4.5	2.9	3.7	3	3.4
C. Faculty as a whole	9.1	4.4	7.4	6	6.1	4.5	5.9	3.7	15	7.4
D. President.......	31.8	26.5	14.8	0	19.4	27.2	35.3	33.3	42	35.4
E. Stand. committee	4.5	8.8	11.1	3	7.4	4.5	16.7	22.2	33	19.4
F. State board.....	41.0	10.3	11.1	6	14.1	4.5	10.3	0	0	5.4
3. Assigning classrooms to instructors										
A. Dean of college	4.5	23.5	29.6	21	21.4	4.5	1.5	3.1	6	3.4
B. Director of instruction..........	4.5	2.9	7.4	3	4.1	4.5	1.5	0	0	1.4
C. Head of department..............	0	1.5	0	6	2.0	0	4.4	7.4	3	4.1
D. President.......	77.2	19.1	11.1	12	24.8	9.1	11.8	7.4	6	9.4
E. Registrar.......	9.1	16.7	22.2	27	18.7	9.1	2.9	3.7	12	6.1
F. Stand. committee	0	7.5	3.7	6	5.4	0	1.5	3.1	6	2.8
G. Vice president...	0	5.9	0	6	4.1	0	0	0	0	0
4. Assigning faculty members to teach various approved courses										
A. Dean of college	4.5	16.7	18.5	6	12.8	4.5	7.5	18.5	18	11.4
B. Director of instruction..........	4.5	0	3.7	0	1.4	4.5	2.9	3.7	3	3.4
C. Head of department..............	0	4.4	22.2	21	10.7	0	8.8	11.1	39	14.8
D. President.......	77.2	36.8	22.2	15	35.4	13.6	29.4	22.2	36	27.4
E. Registrar.......	0	11.5	3.7	3	2.0	0	10.3	3.7	3	6.1
F. Stand. committee	0	2.9	3.7	0	2.0	0	2.9	3.7	0	2.0

TABLE XXIII—(*Continued*)

Functions and Chief Administrative Officers and Groups Who Usually Perform Them	Percentage of Colleges in Which One Officer or Group Usually Performs the Administrative Function					Percentage of Colleges in Which Two or More Officers or Groups Usually Cooperate in Performing the Function				
	Enrollment					Enrollment				
	Under 300	300 to 799	800 to 1199	1200 or More	All Colleges Combined	Under 300	300 to 799	800 to 1199	1200 or More	All Colleges Combined
5. Construction and revision of curricula										
A. Dean of the college.............	4.5	1.5	11.1	0	3.4	9.1	11.8	25.9	27	17.4
B. Director of instruction..........	0	0	3.7	3	1.4	4.5	2.9	3.7	9	4.8
C. Faculty as a whole	4.5	2.9	3.7	3	3.4	18.2	13.2	11.1	18	13.4
D. Head of department..............	0	0	0	3	.7	18.2	13.2	11.1	18	14.8
E. President.......	9.1	2.9	0	3	3.4	50.0	30.9	25.9	24	31.4
F. Standing committee...............	13.6	16.7	14.8	12	14.8	4.5	19.1	25.9	36	22.0
G. State board.....	22.7	13.2	11.1	3	12.0	9.1	5.9	2.7	3	5.4
6. Determining required courses for various certificates and degrees										
A. Dean of the college.............	4.5	0	0	3	1.4	13.6	10.3	22.2	21	15.4
B. Faculty as a whole	4.5	2.9	0	3	2.8	9.1	7.5	0	21	9.4
C. Faculty council..	0	2.9	3.7	6	3.4	4.5	5.9	7.4	18	8.7
D. President.......	9.1	2.9	0	3	3.4	27.2	26.5	22.2	21	24.8
E. Standing committee...............	9.1	13.2	18.5	3	10.0	9.1	13.2	14.8	21	14.8
F. State board.....	36.3	27.9	22.2	15	25.4	9.1	13.2	11.1	3	10.0
7. Formulating policies concerning campus instruction										
A. Dean of the college.............	4.5	1.5	3.7	3	2.8	9.1	16.7	29.6	30	20.7
B. Director of instruction..........	0	0	0	0	0	4.5	5.9	7.4	12	7.4
C. Faculty council..	0	5.9	11.1	6	6.1	0	5.9	0	15	10.0
D. President.......	31.8	19.1	22.2	3	18.1	59.0	44.1	33.3	39	43.4
E. Standing committee...............	4.5	7.5	14.8	6	8.1	4.5	13.2	11.1	12	11.4
8. Formulating rules and regulations concerning the use of the library										
A. Dean of the college.............	4.5	0	0	0	.7	4.5	5.9	7.4	9	6.7
B. Faculty council..	0	1.5	0	3	1.4	0	4.4	7.4	3	4.1
C. Librarian.......	22.7	29.4	44.4	21	29.4	50.0	52.9	44.4	54	51.4
D. President.......	13.6	1.5	30.0	0	2.8	50.0	35.3	33.3	33	36.7
E. Standing committee...............	4.5	4.4	7.4	3	4.8	9.1	8.8	14.8	24	13.4

TABLE XXIII—(*Continued*)

Functions and Chief Administrative Officers and Groups Who Usually Perform Them	Percentage of Colleges in Which One Officer or Group Usually Performs the Administrative Function					Percentage of Colleges in Which Two or More Officers or Groups Usually Cooperate in Performing the Function				
	Enrollment					Enrollment				
	Under 300	300 to 799	800 to 1199	1200 or More	All Colleges Combined	Under 300	300 to 799	800 to 1199	1200 or More	All Colleges Combined
9. Keeping the teaching and extracurricular load balanced for the instructional staff										
A. Dean of the college	4.5	13.2	33.3	12	15.4	4.5	8.8	18.5	24	13.4
B. Director of instruction	0	1.5	3.7	3	2.0	0	4.4	3.7	9	4.8
C. Head of department	4.5	1.5	3.7	3	1.4	4.5	4.4	20.0	12	5.4
D. President	54.5	23.5	22.2	18	26.7	21.8	41.2	22.2	39	36.1
E. Standing committee	0	4.4	7.4	3	4.1	4.5	4.4	7.4	3	4.8
10. Planning facilities for student-teaching										
A. Dean of the college	4.5	4.4	3.7	0	3.4	4.5	5.9	18.5	15	10.0
B. Director of training	22.7	41.2	29.6	36	35.4	41.0	27.9	48.1	39	36.1
C. El. school principal	4.5	0	0	0	.7	9.1	10.3	14.8	6	10.0
D. High school principal	4.5	0	0	0	.7	9.1	1.5	14.8	3	5.4
E. President	9.1	2.9	3.7	6	4.8	54.5	29.4	22.2	15	28.7
F. Vice-president	0	0	0	0	0	0	5.9	0	0	2.8
11. Planning integration of theory and practice										
A. Dean of the college	4.5	5.9	7.4	6	6.1	13.6	11.8	22.2	15	14.8
B. Director of training	4.5	19.1	18.5	18	16.7	45.4	33.3	37.0	39	38.1
C. El. school principal	4.5	1.5	0	3	2.0	4.5	11.8	7.4	6	8.7
D. High school principal	4.5	1.5	0	3	2.0	4.5	13.2	7.4	3	8.7
E. Head of department	4.5	1.5	0	3	2.0	4.5	13.2	14.8	18	13.4
F. President	18.2	1.5	3.7	3	4.8	45.4	30.9	18.5	21	26.7
G. Standing committee	4.5	4.4	7.4	3	4.8	9.1	4.4	0	3	4.1
12. Planning improvement of library service										
A. Dean of the college	4.5	0	0	0	.7	4.5	8.8	7.4	6	7.4
B. Librarian	27.2	25.0	51.8	27	30.7	50.0	55.9	33.3	45	48.7

TABLE XXIII—(*Continued*)

Functions and Chief Administrative Officers and Groups Who Usually Perform Them	Percentage of Colleges in Which One Officer or Group Usually Performs the Administrative Function					Percentage of Colleges in Which Two or More Officers or Groups Usually Cooperate in Performing the Function				
	Enrollment					Enrollment				
	Under 300	300 to 799	800 to 1199	1200 or More	All Colleges Combined	Under 300	300 to 799	800 to 1199	1200 or More	All Colleges Combined
12. (*Cont'd.*)										
C. President.......	9.1	1.5	0	0	2.0	54.5	44.1	29.6	24	38.7
D. Standing committee..............	9.1	2.9	11.1	6	6.1	9.1	10.3	3.7	9	8.7
13. Planning programs for assemblies										
A. Dean of the college..............	4.5	1.5	11.1	3	4.1	4.5	1.5	3.7	15	5.4
B. President.......	27.2	7.5	18.5	15	11.4	22.7	17.6	14.8	30	20.7
C. Special committee	9.1	22.1	18.5	9	16.7	9.1	5.9	3.7	3	5.4
D. Standing committee..............	45.4	25.0	29.6	15	26.7	10.2	5.9	0	6	6.7
E. Student council..	0	4.4	0	6	3.4	0	7.5	7.4	15	8.1
14. Planning programs for special occasions										
A. Dean of the college..............	4.5	1.5	0	0	1.4	4.5	4.4	7.4	12	6.7
B. Head of department..............	0	0	3.7	0	.7	4.5	5.9	0	12	6.7
C. President.......	13.6	2.9	3.7	9	6.1	36.3	23.5	11.1	30	24.8
D. Special committee	13.6	30.9	62.9	15	30.7	22.7	11.8	11.1	21	15.4
E. Standing committee..............	18.2	19.1	7.4	18	16.7	13.6	16.7	13.7	9	12.0
15. Planning commencement programs										
A. Dean of the college..............	4.5	4.4	3.7	3	4.1	9.1	10.3	14.8	15	12.0
B. President.......	22.7	19.1	18.5	15	18.7	59.0	48.5	25.9	45	45.4
C. Special committee	13.6	14.7	25.9	12	16.1	9.1	14.7	7.4	9	11.4
D. Standing committee..............	18.2	13.2	25.9	18	17.4	13.6	7.5	3.7	18	10.0
16. Providing a schedule for final examinations										
A. Dean of the college..............	4.5	23.5	11.1	21	18.1	4.5	5.9	14.8	15	9.4
B. President.......	9.1	7.5	0	0	4.8	31.8	2.9	3.7	6	8.1
C. Registrar.......	9.1	14.7	18.5	12	14.1	22.7	7.5	18.5	12	12.8
D. Standing committee..............	13.6	5.9	14.8	3	8.1	4.5	4.4	0	3	3.4
E. Vice-president...	0	5.9	0	3	3.4	0	1.5	0	3	1.4
17. Providing for substitution in case of faculty absence										
A. Dean of the college..............	4.5	22.1	14.8	12	16.1	9.1	5.9	25.9	21	13.4

TABLE XXIII—*(Continued)*

Functions and Chief Administrative Officers and Groups Who Usually Perform Them	Percentage of Colleges in Which One Officer or Group Usually Performs the Administrative Function					Percentage of Colleges in Which Two or More Officers or Groups Usually Cooperate in Performing the Function				
	Enrollment					Enrollment				
	Under 300	300 to 799	800 to 1199	1200 or More	All Colleges Combined	Under 300	300 to 799	800 to 1199	1200 or More	All Colleges Combined
17. *(Cont'd.)*										
B. Head of department..............	0	0	14.8	18	6.7	0	0	14.8	33	10.0
C. President.......	54.5	33.8	29.6	15	32.0	31.8	22.7	25.9	18	23.4
D. Vice-president...	0	5.9	0	3	3.4	0	1.5	0	6	2.0
18. Providing a time schedule for courses to be offered										
A. Dean of college	9.1	17.6	25.9	21	18.7	0	8.8	7.4	9	7.4
B. President.......	36.3	4.4	0	0	7.4	27.2	25.0	11.1	9	19.4
C. Registrar.......	13.6	11.8	11.1	21	14.1	18.2	4.4	11.1	18	10.7
D. Stand. committee	18.2	11.8	22.2	6	13.4	4.5	5.9	0	9	5.4
E. Vice-president...	0	4.4	0	3	1.4	0	4.4	0	3	2.8
19. Selecting library books										
A. Faculty as a whole	18.2	2.9	0	3	4.8	18.2	16.7	22.2	21	18.7
B. Head of department..............	4.5	8.8	3.7	9	7.4	13.6	30.9	37.0	27	28.7
C. Librarian.......	9.1	13.2	14.8	21	14.8	41.0	50.0	59.2	48	50.0
D. President.......	4.5	5.9	0	0	3.4	36.3	11.8	18.5	3	14.8
E. Stand. committee	9.1	2.9	14.8	3	6.1	4.5	7.5	14.8	18	10.7
20. Supervising the instruction of the probationary members of the staff										
A. Dean of college	4.5	7.5	11.1	6	7.4	4.5	8.8	3.7	18	9.4
B. Director of instruction..........	4.5	2.9	3.7	6	4.1	4.5	1.5	3.7	3	2.8
C. Head of department..............	0	5.9	22.2	21	11.4	4.5	11.8	3.7	27	12.8
D. President.......	45.4	23.5	0	0	17.4	13.6	19.1	3.7	18	15.4
E. Vice-president...	0	1.5	0	0	.7	0	1.5	0	0	.7
21. Supervising the coordination of the various instructional departments										
A. Dean of the college..............	9.1	13.2	22.2	24	16.7	0	11.8	22.2	12	12.0
B. Director of instruction..........	4.5	4.4	7.4	6	5.4	4.5	4.4	0	6	4.1
C. President.......	50.0	29.4	14.8	18	27.4	27.2	17.6	25.9	12	19.1
D. Faculty as a whole	0	2.9	11.1	0	3.4	0	5.9	3.7	6	4.8
22. Supervising the maintenance of scholarship standards										
A. Dean of the college..............	13.6	10.3	14.8	18	13.4	4.5	7.5	22.2	24	14.8

TABLE XXIII—(*Continued*)

Functions and Chief Administrative Officers and Groups Who Usually Perform Them	Percentage of Colleges in Which One Officer or Group Usually Performs the Administrative Function					Percentage of Colleges in Which Two or More Officers or Groups Usually Cooperate in Performing the Function				
	Enrollment					Enrollment				
	Under 300	300 to 799	800 to 1199	1200 or More	All Colleges Combined	Under 300	300 to 799	800 to 1199	1200 or More	All Colleges Combined
22. (*Cont'd.*)										
B. Director of instruction..........	4.5	1.5	0	3	2.0	9.1	8.8	0	9	3.4
C. Faculty as a whole	4.5	5.9	3.1	0	4.1	13.6	20.6	3.7	6	5.4
D. President.......	22.7	11.8	22.2	3	13.4	22.7	22.1	11.1	21	20.7
E. Standing committee...............	13.6	7.5	11.1	6	8.7	9.1	10.3	3.7	12	9.4
F. Vice-president...	0	1.5	0	0	.7	0		0	3	4.1
23. Recommending courses to be offered by the department concerned										
A. Dean of the college..............	4.5	5.9	0	3	4.1	4.5	7.5	7.4	12	8.1
B. Faculty as a whole	4.5	0	0	0	.7	13.6	8.8	7.4	9	9.4
C. Head of department..............	27.2	35.3	66.6	60	45.4	9.1	20.6	14.8	21	18.1
D. President.......	9.1	4.4	0	0	3.4	18.2	22.1	7.4	0	14.1
E. Standing committee...............	4.5	4.4	3.7	3	3.4	4.5	10.3	7.4	9	8.7
24. Recommending requirements for department majors and minors										
A. Dean of the college..............	4.5	5.9	3.7	0	3.4	9.1	10.3	14.8	12	11.4
B. Head of department..............	18.2	26.5	33.3	48	31.4	13.6	17.6	22.2	30	20.7
C. President.......	9.1	2.9	0	0	2.8	4.5	16.7	7.4	6	10.7
D. Standing committee...............	4.5	2.9	14.8	3	5.4	9.1	14.7	3.7	27	14.8
E. State board.....	4.5	5.9	0	3	4.1	4.5	5.9	0	6	4.8
25. Recommending a time schedule for departmental courses										
A. Dean of the college..............	4.5	8.8	14.8	3	8.1	4.5	10.3	7.4	9	8.7
B. Head of department..............	18.2	23.5	40.7	45	30.7	13.6	14.7	3.7	18	13.4
C. President.......	18.2	2.9	0	0	4.1	9.1	11.8	3.7	3	8.1
D. Standing committee...............	4.5	5.9	14.8	3	6.7	4.5	8.8	3.7	6	6.7

This table should be read as follows: Full responsibility for approving policies concerning campus instruction is delegated to the dean of the college by none of the colleges enrolling fewer than 300 students; by 5.9% of the colleges enrolling 300–799; by 7.4% of the colleges enrolling 800–1199; and by 6% of the colleges enrolling 1200 or more students. In cooperation with other officers this responsibility is delegated to the dean of the college by 9.1% of the colleges enrolling under 300, etc.

Consult page 89 for a statement concerning the interpretation of data in this table.

Directors of training are limited chiefly to two functions in campus instruction. These are: planning facilities for student teaching and planning integration of theory and practice. In all but the small institutions these functions are delegated to directors of training more frequently than to any other officers. To the casual observer it might seem that these two functions would not give the director of training an important part in campus instruction. However, when one considers that student teaching involves all the professional and professionalized subject matter courses, it is clear that these two functions are far-reaching in their influence and scope within the institution, and probably of sufficient size and importance to challenge the best energy and ability of any official.

The faculty as a whole and as groups are used in many institutions to control and direct instructional functions. Constructing and revising curricula, determining required courses for various certificates and degrees, selecting library books, and recommending courses to be offered by various departments are functions frequently performed by the faculty as a whole. Standing committees are often used to approve new courses, to construct and revise curricula, to determine requirements for certificates and degrees, to formulate rules and regulations concerning the use of the library, and to plan improvement of library service. Planning programs for assemblies, special occasions, and commencements are in many institutions functions of either special or standing committees.

The faculty council in a few institutions cooperates in determining required courses for certificates and degrees and in formulating rules and regulations for library service. Since these functions are policy-making and since other functions are not assigned to the faculty council, it is probably safe to assume that the faculty council is not used to administer functions regarding instruction.

The state board of control retains direction of the curricula in some institutions, more particularly the smaller ones. The state board, through its experts, frequently constructs and revises the curricula, determines required courses for various certificates and degrees, approves policies concerning campus instruction, and recommends requirements for department majors and minors. However, it is evident that the larger the institution, the less likely it is that the state board will retain control of these curricular functions.

EXTENSION INSTRUCTION

Two dominant facts stand out in Table XXIV, page 112. The most striking of these facts is the low percentages of the institutions which report the performance of administrative functions concerning extension instruction. Reports from the 150 institutions investigated show that fifty-three of these colleges have no extension instruction of any kind. Eighty-nine of them offer no courses by correspondence. It is quite obvious that a few institutions can contribute to the needs of teachers who desire to study by correspondence regardless of where those institutions may be located. On the other hand, the organization of extension classes is largely limited by the geographical location of the institutions concerned. A careful examination of the data which were not tabulated shows that the smaller institutions tend toward eliminating extension instruction of both correspondence and extension-class type, and that of the larger institutions those located in the more densely populated districts will be more likely to have extension-class instruction. The second dominant fact in Table XXIV is the prevailing practice of all institutions, regardless of size, to delegate practically all functions relating to extension instruction to the director of extension. The data indicate very few institutions delegating functions to one of the older established offices. The predominant practice is for the director of extension to have responsibility in all functions except the approval of policies which, as a rule, is retained largely by the president. The director of extension formulates policies, organizes and enrolls students in extension classes, determines what courses may be offered by correspondence, edits correspondence courses, and enrolls students for correspondence study. He supervises the grading of correspondence students. The director also prepares publicity material and serves as a clearing-house agency for problems arising which affect extension students and their instructors.

These data indicate the possibility of a system of extension instruction growing up within an institution quite independent of

TABLE XXIV

EXTENSION INSTRUCTION

THE PERFORMANCE OF ADMINISTRATIVE FUNCTIONS IN 22 SMALL, 68 MEDIUM
SIZED, 27 LARGE, AND 33 EXTRA LARGE TEACHERS COLLEGES. 1932

Functions and Chief Administrative Officers and Groups Who Usually Perform Them	Percentage of Colleges in Which One Officer or Group Usually Performs the Administrative Function					Percentage of Colleges in Which Two or More Officers or Groups Usually Cooperate in Performing the Function				
	Enrollment					Enrollment				
	Under 300	300 to 799	800 to 1199	1200 or More	All Colleges Combined	Under 300	300 to 799	800 to 1199	1200 or More	All Colleges Combined
1. Formulating policies concerning extension instruction										
A. Dean of the college..............	4.5	1.5	0	3	2.0	4.5	7.5	11.1	12	8.7
B. Director of extension..............	4.5	8.8	18.5	24	12.0	9.1	17.6	25.9	36	22.0
C. President.......	9.1	1.5	0	3	2.8	9.1	25.0	25.9	30	24.1
D. Standing committee................	4.5	1.5	11.1	0	3.4	0	8.8	3.7	30	11.4
E. State board.....	13.6	7.5	3.7	3	6.7	13.6	1.5	3.7	3	4.1
2. Approving policies concerning extension instruction										
A. Dean of the college..............	0	1.5	0	0	.7	9.1	4.4	18.5	15	10.0
B. Director of extension..............	0	0	3.7	0	.7	9.1	5.9	14.8	18	10.7
C. President.......	9.1	19.1	29.6	18	19.4	18.2	19.1	29.6	36	24.8
D. Standing committee................	4.5	1.5	3.7	0	2.0	0	5.9	11.1	0	7.0
E. State board.....	13.6	7.5	7.4	6	10.0	9.1	4.4	3.7	3	7.0
3. Organizing and enrolling students in extension classes										
A. Dean of the college..............	0	7.5	0	0	3.4	4.5	0	3.7	6	4.0
B. Director of extension..............	18.2	20.6	29.6	57	30.0	4.5	5.9	11.1	9	7.4
C. Head of departments.	0	4.4	0	0	2.0	0	1.5	0	3	1.4
D. Registrar.......	13.6	2.9	7.4	0	4.8	9.1	4.4	11.1	9	7.4
E. State board.....	13.6	2.9	0	0	3.4	4.5	1.5	0	0	1.4
4. Determining what courses may be offered by correspondence										
A. Dean of the college..............	0	1.5	0	0	.7	9.1	5.9	18.5	9	9.4
B. Director of extension..............	0	0	7.4	3	2.0	4.5	13.2	22.2	27	16.7
C. President.......	4.5	1.5	0	3	5.0	4.5	13.2	11.1	9	10.7
D. Standing committee................	4.5	0	3.7	6	2.8	4.5	7.5	3.7	6	6.1

TABLE XXIV—*(Continued)*

Functions and Chief Administrative Officers and Groups Who Usually Perform Them	Percentage of Colleges in Which One Officer or Group Usually Performs the Administrative Function					Percentage of Colleges in Which Two or More Officers or Groups Usually Cooperate in Performing the Function				
	Enrollment					Enrollment				
	Under 300	300 to 799	800 to 1199	1200 or More	All Colleges Combined	Under 300	300 to 799	800 to 1199	1200 or More	All Colleges Combined
5. Editing correspondence courses										
A. Dean of the college	4.5	1.5	0	0	1.4	0	1.5	3.7	3	2.0
B. Director of extension	4.5	7.5	18.5	27	13.4	0	4.4	7.4	9	5.4
C. Head of department	0	0	11.1	12	4.8	0	7.5	7.4	6	6.1
D. President	4.5	0	0	3	1.4	0	4.4	0	3	2.8
6. Enrolling correspondence students										
A. Dean of the college	0	1.5	0	0	.7	0	0	0	0	0
B. Director of extension	9.1	16.7	33.3	45	24.8	0	2.9	11.1	0	3.4
C. President	0	1.5	0	0	.7	0	1.5	0	0	.7
D. Registrar	13.6	2.9	14.8	3	6.7	0	1.5	3.7	0	1.4
7. Supervising the grading of correspondence papers										
A. Director of extension	4.5	13.2	25.9	27	17.4	4.5	1.5	0	12	4.1
B. President	0	1.5	0	3	1.4	0	2.9	0	3	2.0
C. Registrar	0	0	0	0	0	0	0	3.7	0	.7
D. Standing committee	0	1.5	0	0	.7	0	1.5	0	0	.7
8. Supervising correspondence study examinations										
A. Director of extension	9.1	11.8	33.3	33	20.0	0	2.9	3.7	9	4.1
B. Head of department	0	1.5	7.4	3	2.8	0	2.9	3.7	6	3.4
C. President	0	0	0	3	.7	0	4.4	0	3	2.8
D. Standing committee	0	1.5	0	0	.7	0	1.5	0	0	.7
9. Recording grades for extension class students										
A. Dean of the college	0	2.9	0	0	1.4	0	0	3.7	0	.7
B. Director of extension	4.5	7.5	18.5	6	8.7	0	5.9	11.1	12	7.4
C. Registrar	36.3	20.6	37.0	54	33.4	0	4.4	14.8	12	7.4

TABLE XXIV—*(Continued)*

Functions and Chief Administrative Officers and Groups Who Usually Perform Them	Percentage of Colleges in Which One Officer or Group Usually Performs the Administrative Function					Percentage of Colleges in Which Two or More Officers or Groups Usually Cooperate in Performing the Function				
	Enrollment					Enrollment				
	Under 300	300 to 799	800 to 1199	1200 or More	All Colleges Combined	Under 300	300 to 799	800 to 1199	1200 or More	All Colleges Combined
10. Recording grades for correspondence students										
A. Dean of the college..............	0	1.5	0	0	.7	0	0	3.7	0	.7
B. Director of extension..............	4.5	4.4	14.8	9	7.4	0	4.4	11.1	12	6.7
C. Registrar.......	22.7	14.7	22.2	33	21.4	0	2.9	14.8	12	6.7
11. Collecting and accounting for extension fees										
A. Business agent...	9.1	17.6	22.2	15	16.7	13.6	11.8	22.2	18	15.4
B. Director of extension..............	9.1	7.5	22.2	24	14.1	9.1	11.8	18.5	27	16.1
C. Registrar.......	13.6	0	7.4	9	5.4	4.5	0	3.7	3	2.0
12. Preparation of extension publicity material										
A. Dean of the college..............	4.5	1.5	0	3	2.0	0	4.4	0	3	2.8
B. Director of extension..............	13.6	22.1	48.1	36	28.7	4.5	2.9	3.7	15	6.1
C. President.......	4.5	5.9	3.7	3	4.8	9.1	5.9	3.7	6	6.1
D. Registrar.......	9.1	1.5	7.4	6	4.8	9.1	1.5	3.7	0	2.8
13. Serving as a clearing house for extension students and extension instructors										
A. Dean of the college..............	4.5	4.4	3.7	3	4.1	0	1.5	0	6	2.0
B. Director of extension..............	13.6	20.6	37.0	45	28.1	4.5	2.9	0	9	4.1
C. President.......	0	2.9	0	3	2.0	4.5	5.9	0	3	4.1
D. Registrar.......	13.6	0	14.8	3	5.4	4.5	1.5	0	9	3.4

This table should be read as follows: Full responsibility for formulating policies concerning extension instruction is delegated to the dean of the college by 4.5% of the colleges enrolling fewer than 300 students; by 1.5% of the colleges enrolling 300–799; by none of the colleges enrolling 800–1199; and by 3% of the colleges enrolling 1200 or more students. In cooperation with other officers this responsibility is delegated to the dean of the college by 4.5% of the colleges enrolling under 300, etc.

Consult page 89 for a statement concerning the interpretation of data in this table.

the standards which may govern instruction on the campus unless the president is consciously aware of the danger involved in such an organization and strives continually to keep the standards for extension instruction equally as high as those which govern instruction on the campus.

EDUCATIONAL RESEARCH

It is evident from Table XXV, page 116, that educational research in teachers colleges receives less attention than some other groups of functions. The low percentages of institutions delegating research functions to one officer or to two or more, indicate that many teachers colleges do not have a program of research. The president, regardless of the size of the institution, is on the whole the dominant figure in research as carried forward by teachers colleges. With the exception of actually conducting the research projects, the president reserves research functions to himself in greater percentages than he delegates them. He, in cooperation with others, largely the dean and heads of departments, formulates policies concerning research. He approves research policies and decides what research is most needed; and by far in the largest number of cases, he decides what to do with research findings.

The conducting of research projects is performed in a number of ways. In institutions under 300 in enrollment, a few presidents conduct research, a few others delegate the research projects to committees; but in most of the small institutions no research projects are reported. In the larger institutions research projects are delegated to directors of research, to heads of departments, and to committees, with cooperation from deans and presidents.

A comparison of Table VI, page 52, and Table XXV raises some questions difficult to answer. Directors of research are reported in 18 per cent of the institutions included in the study. Yet when it comes to performing the function of formulation of policies concerning research, only 11 per cent of the total number of colleges use this officer to help formulate policies. In conducting research projects, only 13 per cent of the institutions use their director of research. A possible explanation of this seeming contradiction is that some institutions include their

TABLE XXV

EDUCATIONAL RESEARCH

THE PERFORMANCE OF ADMINISTRATIVE FUNCTIONS IN 22 SMALL, 68 MEDIUM SIZED, 27 LARGE, AND 33 EXTRA LARGE TEACHERS COLLEGES. 1932

Functions and Chief Administrative Officers and Groups Who Usually Perform Them	Percentage of Colleges in Which One Officer or Group Usually Performs the Administrative Function					Percentage of Colleges in Which Two or More Officers or Groups Usually Cooperate in Performing the Function				
	Enrollment					Enrollment				
	Under 300	300 to 799	800 to 1199	1200 or More	All Colleges Combined	Under 300	300 to 799	800 to 1199	1200 or More	All Colleges Combined
1. Formulating policies concerning institutional research										
A. Dean of the college...............	0	0	3.7	3	1.4	0	8.8	3.7	15	8.1
B. Director of research.............	0	4.4	3.7	6	4.1	0	4.4	11.1	12	6.7
C. Head of department..............	0	1.5	0	3	1.4	4.5	8.8	14.8	18	11.4
D. President.......	9.1	1.5	0	3	2.8	22.7	26.5	22.2	36	27.4
E. Standing committee................	4.5	1.5	7.4	9	5.4	4.5	44.0	3.7	9	3.4
2. Approving policies concerning institutional research										
A. Dean of the college...............	0	0	0	0	0	0	7.5	7.4	6	6.1
B. Director of research.............	0	0	0	3	7	0	0	11.1	9	4.1
C. President.......	22.7	75	18.5	30	7.4	27.2	27.9	18.5	30	24.1
D. Standing committee................	0	0	0	6	4.8	13.6	2.9	3.7	3	7.4
3. Deciding what research is most needed										
A. Dean of the college...............	0	0	3.7	0	.7	0	8.8	7.4	9	7.4
B. Director of research.............	0	0	3.7	3	1.4	0	2.9	11.1	12	6.1
C. Head of department..............	0	1.5	0	0	.7	4.5	8.8	11.1	12	9.4
D. President.......	18.2	13.2	0	21	13.4	13.6	27.9	18.5	39	26.7
4. Deciding what to do with research findings										
A. Dean of the college...............	0	0	0	0	0	0	8.8	11.1	9	8.1
B. Director of research.............	0	0	3.7	3	1.4	0	8.8	7.4	9	6.7
C. Head of department..............	0	1.5	0	3	1.4	0	4.1	14.8	15	8.1
D. President.......	22.7	10.3	7.4	24	14.8	18.2	27.9	18.5	36	26.7

TABLE XXV—(*Continued*)

Functions and Chief Administrative Officers and Groups Who Usually Perform Them	Percentage of Colleges in Which One Officer or Group Usually Performs the Administrative Function					Percentage of Colleges in Which Two or More Officers or Groups Usually Cooperate in Performing the Function				
	Enrollment					Enrollment				
	Under 300	300 to 799	800 to 1199	1200 or More	All Colleges Combined	Under 300	300 to 799	800 to 1199	1200 or More	All Colleges Combined
5. Conducting research projects										
A. Dean of the college..............	0	0	0	0	0	0	2.9	7.4	18	6.7
B. Director of research............	0	7.5	7.4	21	9.4	0	1.5	11.1	6	4.1
C. Head of department.............	0	5.9	3.7	3	4.1	0	4.4	18.5	21	10.0
D. President.......	4.5	4.4	0	0	2.8	9.1	7.5	7.4	9	8.1
E. Registrar.......	0	1.5	0	0	.7	0	1.5	7.4	21	6.7
F. Standing committee..............	4.5	13.2	14.8	9	11.4	4.5	7.5	7.4	3	6.1

This table should be read as follows: Full responsibility for formulating policies concerning institutional research is delegated to the dean of the college by none of the colleges enrolling fewer than 300 students; by none of the colleges enrolling 300–799; by 3.7% of the colleges enrolling 800–1199; by 3% of the colleges enrolling 1200 or more students. In cooperation with other officers this responsibility is delegated to the dean of the college by none of the colleges enrolling under 300, etc.
Consult page 89 for a statement concerning interpretation of the data in this table.

directors of research as members of committees and use their services there in formulating policies and in conducting research projects. Table XXV shows that none of the small colleges reports the dean as sharing in any way in research. Table VI shows that 31.8 per cent of the small colleges have deans. Naturally the question arises why they have nothing to do with research. The most plausible answer is that research projects are not conducted in small teachers colleges. This assumption is supported by the fact that approximately only 14 per cent of the small colleges report that research functions are performed by anyone.

FACULTY PERSONNEL RELATIONS

Those administrative functions in a teachers college which concern the personnel relations of the members of the faculty are in nearly all cases under the immediate direction and control of the presidents. Table XXVI, page 118, shows that the

TABLE XXVI

FACULTY PERSONNEL RELATIONS

THE PERFORMANCE OF ADMINISTRATIVE FUNCTIONS IN 22 SMALL, 68 MEDIUM SIZED, 27 LARGE, AND 33 EXTRA LARGE TEACHERS COLLEGES. 1932

Functions and Chief Administrative Officers and Groups Who Usually Perform Them	Percentage of Colleges in Which One Officer or Group Usually Performs the Administrative Function					Percentage of Colleges in Which Two or More Officers or Groups Usually Cooperate in Performing the Function				
	Enrollment					Enrollment				
	Under 300	300 to 799	800 to 1199	1200 or More	All Colleges Combined	Under 300	300 to 799	800 to 1199	1200 or More	All Colleges Combined
1. Formulating policies concerning faculty personnel relations										
A. Dean of the college	4.5	2.9	0	3	2.8	4.5	5.9	25.9	15	11.4
B. Faculty as a whole	4.5	0	0	0	.7	13.6	2.9	0	3	4.1
C. President	59.0	38.2	33.3	15	32.0	22.7	27.9	40.7	36	31.4
D. State board	4.5	1.5	3.7	3	2.8	4.5	1.5	7.4	3	3.4
2. Approving policies concerning faculty personnel relations										
A. Dean of the college	4.5	0	0	0	.7	4.5	2.9	7.4	6	4.8
B. President	63.6	51.5	59.2	45	53.4	9.1	13.2	14.8	21	14.8
C. State board	13.6	2.9	11.1	3	6.1	4.5	4.4	3.7	3	4.1
3. Locating desirable candidates for positions										
A. Dean of the college	4.5	1.5	0	3	2.0	4.5	7.5	18.5	9	9.4
B. Head of department	4.5	0	0	0	.7	4.5	20.6	44.4	39	26.7
C. President	59.0	55.9	37.0	24	46.1	22.7	32.3	55.5	51	39.4
D. State board	4.5	1.5	0	0	1.4	9.1	1.5	0	0	2.0
4. Offering contracts to prospective staff members										
A. Head of department	0	0	0	0	0	0	4.4	0	9	4.1
B. President	63.6	69.1	85.1	66	70.7	18.2	14.7	7.4	18	14.8
C. State board	4.5	7.5	0	3	4.8	9.1	5.9	3.7	6	6.1
5. Determining academic ranking of staff members										
A. Dean of college	4.5	0	3.7	0	1.4	4.5	2.9	11.1	9	6.1
B. President	45.4	50.0	59.2	72	36.1	13.6	13.2	18.8	21	16.1
C. State board	9.1	7.5	7.4	0	6.1	4.5	4.4	0	0	2.8

TABLE XXVI—(*Continued*)

Functions and Chief Administrative Officers and Groups Who Usually Perform Them	Percentage of Colleges in Which One Officer or Group Usually Performs the Administrative Function					Percentage of Colleges in Which Two or More Officers or Groups Usually Cooperate in Performing the Function				
	Enrollment					Enrollment				
	Under 300	300 to 799	800 to 1199	1200 or More	All Colleges Combined	Under 300	300 to 799	800 to 1199	1200 or More	All Colleges Combined
6. Planning staff insurance and retirement funds										
A. Faculty as a whole	4.5	4.4	0	3	3.4	4.5	0	0	3	1.4
B. President........	9.1	8.8	7.4	12	9.4	9.1	7.5	7.4	18	10.0
C. Standing committee...............	0	2.9	0	9	3.4	0	2.9	3.7	3	2.8
D. State board.....	31.8	17.6	0	6	14.1	0	5.9	7.4	6	5.4
7. Determining eligibility for leave of absence of staff members										
A. President........	45.4	47.0	66.6	63	54.1	13.6	8.8	11.1	12	10.7
B. State board.....	13.6	10.3	0	6	8.1	13.6	8.8	0	6	7.4
8. Planning in-service training for staff members										
A. Dean of the college...............	4.5	1.5	7.4	3	3.4	4.5	4.4	14.8	12	8.1
B. Head of department..............	0	1.5	3.7	3	2.4	0	4.4	3.7	21	7.4
C. President........	63.6	32.3	29.6	27	35.4	9.1	22.1	22.2	39	24.1
D. State board.....	4.5	2.9	3.7	3	3.4	4.5	5.9	3.7	3	4.8
9. Planning social affairs to build faculty acquaintanceship										
A. Dean of college..	0	0	0	0	0	0	7.5	7.4	6	6.1
B. Dean of men....	0	1.5	0	0	.7	4.5	10.3	3.7	0	6.1
C. Dean of women..	13.6	2.9	11.1	6	6.7	13.6	13.2	11.1	6	11.4
D. President........	13.6	2.9	14.8	9	8.1	22.7	22.1	18.1	9	18.7
E. Standing committee...............	18.2	44.1	25.9	42	36.7	4.5	11.8	14.8	18	12.8
10. Planning adequate housing facilities for staff members										
A. Business manager	0	0	3.7	0	.7	0	4.4	0	3	2.8
B. President........	13.6	5.9	14.8	9	9.4	0	16.7	3.7	6	9.4
C. State board.....	4.3	0	0	0	.7	4.5	2.9	0	0	2.0
11. Arranging exchange professorships in other institutions										
A. President........	4.5	11.8	29.6	21	16.1	0	4.4	0	6	3.4
B. State board.....	0	0	0	0	0	0	1.5	0	0	.7
C. Standing committee...............	0	0	0	0	0	0	0	0	0	0

TABLE XXVI—(*Continued*)

Functions and Chief Administrative Officers and Groups Who Usually Perform Them	Percentage of Colleges in Which One Officer or Group Usually Performs the Administrative Function					Percentage of Colleges in Which Two or More Officers or Groups Usually Cooperate in Performing the Function				
	Enrollment					Enrollment				
	Under 300	300 to 799	800 to 1199	1200 or More	All Colleges Combined	Under 300	300 to 799	800 to 1199	1200 or More	All Colleges Combined
12. Recommending to the president persons to be employed in the department										
A. Dean of the college...............	4.5	2.9	3.7	0	2.8	0	4.4	3.7	18	6.7
B. Head of department.............	27.2	39.7	59.2	57	45.4	0	20.6	11.1	21	16.1
C. Special committee	0	0	0	0	0	0	0	0	0	0
13. Recommending salary changes for all members in the department below the head										
A. Dean of the college...............	0	0	0	0	0	0	2.9	7.4	9	4.8
B. Head of department.............	4.5	7.5	14.8	21	11.4	4.5	11.8	18.5	15	12.8
C. President.......	54.5	42.6	51.8	39	45.4	4.5	14.7	11.1	15	12.8

This table should be read as follows: Full responsibility for formulating policies concerning faculty personnel relations is delegated to the dean of the college by 4.5% of the colleges enrolling fewer than 300 students; by 2.9% of the colleges enrolling 300–799; by none of the colleges enrolling 800–1199; and by 3% of the colleges enrolling 1200 or more students. In cooperation with other officers this responsibility is delegated to the dean of the college by 4.5% of the colleges enrolling under 300, etc. Consult page 89 for a statement concerning the interpretation of data in this table.

presidents tend to retain ten out of thirteen of the functions which primarily affect the personnel relations of staff members. This is true of all colleges regardless of size. The three functions not retained by the presidents are:

1. Planning staff insurance and retirement funds.
2. Planning social affairs to build faculty acquaintanceship.
3. Recommending to the president persons to be employed in the department.

State boards of control retain the functions concerning insurance and retirement funds more frequently than do other individuals or groups. Department heads recommend persons for employment within the departments, and standing committees plan social affairs for the various faculties.   Those functions most frequently performed by the president are:

1. Formulating policies concerning faculty personnel relations.
2. Approving such policies when he does not formulate them.
3. Locating desirable candidates for positions.
4. Offering contracts to prospective staff members.
5. Determining academic ranking of staff members.
6. Determining eligibility for leave of absence.
7. Planning in-service training for staff members.
8. Planning adequate housing facilities for staff members.
9. Arranging exchange professorships.
10. Recommending salary changes.

Other officers participate in the control and direction of faculty personnel relations in a few institutions.   The college dean is now and then delegated the responsibility of locating desirable candidates for positions.   He cooperates in determining academic rank and in planning in-service training for staff members.   In no institution is the dean alone responsible for planning social affairs for the faculty, but some presidents delegate this function to him in cooperation with other officers. Some presidents depend upon the dean for recommending prospective staff members and in determining salary changes.   The deans of men and deans of women help in faculty social functions but have little to do with other faculty personnel relations.

The small percentages of institutions which report the performance of functions relating to providing for staff insurance, arranging housing facilities for staff members, and financing exchange professorships indicate that these functions are neglected in a large number of teachers colleges.   It seems reasonable to assume that these functions are as important in one institution as in another.   If some institutions get worth-while results by attention to them, then others would probably benefit by fixing responsibility for their performance upon some member in the administrative group.

PLACEMENT AND ADJUSTMENT SERVICE

An analysis of Table XXVII, page 122, shows that the director of placement more than any other official performs those

TABLE XXVII

PLACEMENT AND ADJUSTMENT SERVICE

THE PERFORMANCE OF ADMINISTRATIVE FUNCTIONS IN 22 SMALL, 68 MEDIUM SIZED, 27 LARGE, AND 33 EXTRA LARGE TEACHERS COLLEGES. 1932

Functions and Chief Administrative Officers and Groups Who Usually Perform Them	Percentage of Colleges in Which One Officer or Group Usually Performs the Administrative Function					Percentage of Colleges in Which Two or More Officers or Groups Usually Cooperate in Performing the Function				
	Enrollment					Enrollment				
	Under 300	300 to 799	800 to 1199	1200 or More	All Colleges Combined	Under 300	300 to 799	800 to 1199	1200 or More	All Colleges Combined
1. Formulating policies concerning placement and adjustment service										
A. Dean of the college.............	4.5	0	3.7	0	1.4	4.5	11.8	7.4	6	8.7
B. Director of placement.............	9.1	11.8	33.3	30	19.4	18.2	20.6	33.3	33	25.4
C. Director of training...............	4.5	4.4	0	0	2.8	13.6	13.2	18.5	9	13.4
D. President.......	31.8	5.9	0	3	8.1	50.0	32.3	18.5	18	29.4
E. Standing committee...............	4.5	10.3	18.5	6	10.0	9.1	5.9	0	15	7.4
2. Approving policies concerning placement and adjustment service										
A. Dean of the college.............	4.5	0	0	0	.7	0	5.9	0	3	3.4
B. Director of placement.............	4.5	2.9	7.4	6	4.8	13.6	10.3	22.2	30	17.4
C. Director of training...............	0	0	0	0	0	9.1	10.3	11.1	3	8.7
D. President.......	50.0	35.3	51.8	39	34.8	31.8	29.4	18.5	39	30.0
E. State board.....	4.5	0	0	3	1.4	4.5	2.9	0	3	2.8
3. Assembling information for use of employers seeking teachers										
A. Dean of the college.............	4.5	2.9	0	0	2.0	0	2.9	3.7	3	2.8
B. Director of placement.............	18.2	29.4	55.5	60	27.4	9.1	10.3	18.5	12	12.0
C. President.......	9.1	2.9	0	0	2.8	22.7	7.5	7.4	3	8.7
D. Registrar.......	18.2	5.9	0	0	5.4	18.2	19.1	7.4	3	13.4
4. Recommending graduates to prospective employers										
A. Dean of the college.............	4.5	0	0	3	1.4	9.1	7.5	0	3	5.4

TABLE XXVII—*(Continued)*

Functions and Chief Administrative Officers and Groups Who Usually Perform Them	Percentage of Colleges in Which One Officer or Group Usually Performs the Administrative Function					Percentage of Colleges in Which Two or More Officers or Groups Usually Cooperate in Performing the Function				
	Enrollment					Enrollment				
	Under 300	300 to 799	800 to 1199	1200 or More	All Colleges Combined	Under 300	300 to 799	800 to 1199	1200 or More	All Colleges Combined
4. *(Cont'd.)*										
B. Director of placement	18.2	17.6	55.5	42	30.0	9.1	17.6	22.2	27	19.4
C. Director of training	9.1	8.8	0	0	5.4	13.6	19.1	11.1	12	15.4
D. President	13.6	2.9	3.7	3	4.8	50.0	29.4	7.4	12	24.8
E. Registrar	4.5	4.4	0	0	2.8	22.7	4.4	0	0	5.4
5. Guiding students in making applications										
A. Dean of the college	4.5	1.5	0	0	1.4	4.5	5.9	0	3	4.1
B. Director of placement	18.2	22.1	55.5	45	32.8	9.1	14.7	18.5	30	18.1
C. Director of training	9.1	8.8	0	3	6.1	13.6	16.7	11.1	9	13.4
D. President	27.2	2.9	0	3	6.1	27.2	11.8	3.7	6	11.4
E. Registrar	0	4.4	0	0	2.0	22.7	7.5	0	0	6.7
6. Arranging interviews between students and prospective employers										
A. Dean of the college	4.5	4.4	0	3	5.4	4.5	2.9	0	3	2.8
B. Director of placement	27.2	23.5	55.5	63	38.7	4.5	10.3	14.8	12	10.7
C. Director of training	13.6	13.2	0	3	8.7	4.5	7.5	3.7	6	6.1
D. President	27.2	5.9	3.7	3	8.1	27.2	14.7	3.7	3	11.4
E. Registrar	0	4.4	0	0	2.0	22.7	5.9	0	0	6.1
7. Conducting educational conferences for graduates who are teaching										
A. Dean of the college	4.5	1.5	0	0	1.4	4.5	2.9	3.7	6	4.1
B. Director of extension	0	7.5	3.7	3	4.8	4.5	5.9	3.7	3	4.8
C. Director of placement	9.1	4.4	14.8	6	7.4	9.1	10.3	3.7	9	8.7
D. President	13.6	2.9	3.7	6	5.4	22.7	13.2	3.7	6	11.4
8. Helping graduates secure better positions from year to year										

TABLE XXVII—(*Continued*)

Functions and Chief Administrative Officers and Groups Who Usually Perform Them	Percentage of Colleges in Which One Officer or Group Usually Performs the Administrative Function					Percentage of Colleges in Which Two or More Officers or Groups Usually Cooperate in Performing the Function				
	Enrollment					Enrollment				
	Under 300	300 to 799	800 to 1199	1200 or More	All Colleges Combined	Under 300	300 to 799	800 to 1199	1200 or More	All Colleges Combined
8. (*Cont'd.*)										
A. Dean of the college	0	0	0	0	0	13.6	2.9	3.7	3	4.8
B. Director of placement	13.6	26.5	55.5	51	35.4	13.6	22.1	8.5	18	19.4
C. President	9.1	7.5	0	0	4.8	50.0	19.1	11.1	6	19.4
D. Registrar	0	2.9	0	0	1.4	18.2	5.9	0	0	54.0
9. Supervising faculty visitation of graduates										
A. Dean of the college	4.5	1.5	0	6	2.8	4.5	1.5	0	3	2.0
B. Director of placement	4.5	5.9	11.1	3	6.1	4.5	2.9	0	0	2.0
C. Director of training	4.5	8.8	0	12	7.4	9.1	5.9	0	3	2.8
D. President	41.0	11.8	14.8	3	14.1	13.6	7.5	3.7	3	6.7
10. Student guidance in selection of courses to meet placement demands										
A. Dean of the college	9.1	4.4	3.7	3	4.8	13.6	13.2	18.5	18	15.4
B. Director of placement	0	4.4	18.5	12	8.7	9.1	13.2	18.5	24	14.8
C. Director of training	4.5	4.4	4.7	3	4.1	18.2	8.8	3.7	3	8.1
D. President	13.6	2.9	0	3	4.1	18.2	5.9	11.1	12	10.0
E. Registrar	0	2.9	0	3	2.0	9.1	8.8	0	12	8.1

This table should be read as follows: Full responsibility for formulating policies concerning placement and adjustment service is delegated to the dean of the college by 4.5% of the colleges enrolling fewer than 300 students; by none of the colleges enrolling 300–799; by 3.7% of the colleges enrolling 800–1199; and by none of the colleges enrolling 1200 or more students. In cooperation with other officers this responsibility is delegated to the dean of the college by 4.5% of the colleges enrolling under 300, etc.

Consult page 89 for a statement concerning interpretation of the data in this table.

functions pertaining to placement and adjustment service. The president, the registrar, and the director of training cooperate, but are only directly responsible in a small percentage of the institutions. Fewer than half of the institutions depend upon any one official to formulate placement policies. This may indicate that presidents look upon the formation of policies concerning placement as a function calling for group judgment. The approval of policies is largely in the hands of the presidents and the directors of placement; although deans, directors of training, and the state board are called upon in some institutions to help approve policies. The registrar and the director of placement are chiefly responsible for assembling information. The registrar has less of this responsibility as the enrollment increases in size. Approximately 30 per cent of the colleges depend upon one official, most frequently the director of placement, to recommend the graduates. The rest of the institutions expect the dean, the registrar, the director of training, and the president to help in getting the qualifications of graduates before prospective employers.

The director of placement has close contact with students in placement service. He guides them in making applications for positions. In a large percentage of the institutions, more especially those with heavy enrollments, the director of placement arranges interviews with prospective employers. This is sometimes done by the director of training, and in some of the smaller institutions, by the president; but the usual practice is for this function to be performed by the director of placement.

Some functions are not performed in the majority of institutions. Educational conferences for graduates who are teaching are reported as being conducted in but few institutions. In those institutions which do conduct conferences it is usually the director of placement and the president who have this responsibility. Faculty visitation to graduates is a function supervised in but few institutions. Small colleges report a greater amount of this service than the larger ones. It is most frequently retained by the president as one of his functions. The small percentage of institutions reporting student guidance in the selection of courses to meet placement demands shows that this function is frequently not performed. The few institutions reporting this service divide the responsibility among the dean of the college, the director of placement, the president, the director of training, and the registrar.

PUBLIC RELATIONS OR GOOD-WILL SERVICE

The outstanding fact shown in Table XXVIII, page 127, is that the president holds himself responsible for doing or directing those activities which mean contacts with individuals and organizations outside the college. The presidents formulate policies alone more frequently than they cooperate with subordinate officers in the performance of the task. The approval of public relations policies is almost entirely restricted to the president. The state board and the faculty as a whole are, according to reports of the presidents, seldom called upon to give approval to policies concerning public relations. This may mean that teachers colleges have no definite public relations policies to submit for approval. On the other hand, it may mean that the presidents consider contacts with people outside the college a part of their job and feel that the making of such contacts is a duty which cannot be delegated.

The presidents, more than any other officials, supervise the contacts of the colleges with the public schools. According to reports from the colleges included in this investigation, the presidents visit the public schools more frequently than any of their subordinate officers. They arrange with public schools for members of the staff to lecture at school assemblies and parent-teacher meetings, to judge debates and oratorical contests, and to render technical service, such as testing programs, school surveys, demonstrations of teaching, and school board conferences. If student groups give community programs, such as plays or concerts, the presidents frequently make the arrangements. In large institutions committees more frequently than the president arrange community programs. In a few institutions heads of departments have this responsibility. Whenever functions concerning contacts off the campus are delegated to an officer, it is usually to the director of extension. Data in Table XXVII warrant the assumption that presidents perform many routine duties which might be delegated. The delegation of these functions should free the president and give him more time for developing administrative policies.

TABLE XXVIII

PUBLIC RELATIONS OR GOOD-WILL SERVICE

THE PERFORMANCE OF ADMINISTRATIVE FUNCTIONS IN 22 SMALL, 68 MEDIUM SIZED, 27 LARGE, AND 33 EXTRA LARGE TEACHERS COLLEGES. 1932

Functions and Chief Administrative Officers and Groups Who Usually Perform Them	Percentage of Colleges in Which One Officer or Group Usually Performs the Administrative Function					Percentage of Colleges in Which Two or More Officers or Groups Usually Cooperate in Performing the Function				
	Enrollment					Enrollment				
	Under 300	300 to 799	800 to 1199	1200 or More	All Colleges Combined	Under 300	300 to 799	800 to 1199	1200 or More	All Colleges Combined
1. Formulating policies concerning public relations										
A. Dean of the college..............	0	0	0	0	0	4.5	4.4	14.8	12	8.7
B. Director of extension..............	0	2.9	3.7	0	2.0	0	0	3.7	6	2.0
C. Faculty as a whole	18.2	5.9	0	0	5.4	13.6	2.9	3.7	0	4.1
D. President.......	27.2	38.2	33.3	30	35.4	27.2	13.2	29.6	33	22.8
2. Approving policies concerning public relations										
A. Faculty as a whole	13.6	2.9	0	0	3.4	0	0	3.7	3	1.4
B. President.......	41.0	55.9	29.4	63	50.7	9.1	5.9	11.1	12	8.7
C. State board.....	4.5	0	0	0	.7	0	1.5	0	0	.7
3. Visitation of public schools										
A. Dean of the college..............	0	0	0	3	.7	0	7.5	11.1	6	6.7
B. Director of extension..............	0	2.9	7.4	3	3.4	0	2.9	3.7	3	2.8
C. Director of training..............	0	4.4	0	12	4.1	13.6	14.7	22.2	15	16.1
D. President.......	22.7	16.7	3.7	12	14.1	27.2	25.0	29.6	12	23.4
E. Standing committee..............	4.5	4.4	3.7	0	3.4	4.5	1.5	3.7	0	2.0
4. Arranging for staff members to lecture at school assemblies, parent-teacher meetings, etc.										
A. Dean of the college..............	4.5	1.5	0	0	1.4	0	4.4	11.1	12	6.7
B. Director of extension..............	4.5	2.9	11.1	15	7.4	9.1	2.9	3.7	6	4.8
C. President.......	36.3	41.2	44.4	15	35.4	31.8	19.1	22.2	24	21.4
D. Standing committee..............	0	5.9	3.7	0	3.4	0	1.5	0	0	.7

TABLE XXVIII—(*Continued*)

Functions and Chief Administrative Officers and Groups Who Usually Perform Them	Percentage of Colleges in Which One Officer or Group Usually Performs the Administrative Function					Percentage of Colleges in Which Two or More Officers or Groups Usually Cooperate in Performing the Function				
	Enrollment					Enrollment				
	Under 300	300 to 799	800 to 1199	1200 or More	All Colleges Combined	Under 300	300 to 799	800 to 1199	1200 or More	All Colleges Combined
5. Organizing alumni associations										
A. Dean of women..	0	0	0	0	0	9.1	1.5	0	6	3.4
B. Director of extension..............	0	2.9	11.1	6	4.8	4.5	1.5	0	0	1.4
C. President.......	18.2	13.2	11.1	9	12.8	41.0	14.7	22.2	12	19.4
D. Standing committee................	9.1	19.1	22.2	21	18.7	4.5	7.5	11.1	3	8.1
E. Alumni secretary	4.5	5.9	3.7	3	4.8	4.5	0	0	3	1.4
6. Planning for faculty off-campus contacts with chambers of commerce, educational associations, etc.										
A. Director of extension..............	0	1.5	11.1	12	5.4	0	1.5	3.7	0	1.4
B. Faculty as a whole	4.5	0	0	0	.7	0	5.9	0	3	3.4
C. President.......	45.4	35.3	33.3	39	37.4	13.6	20.6	3.7	9	14.1
7. Arranging for members of the faculty to render technical service such as surveys, testing programs, demonstration teaching, etc.										
A. Dean of the college..............	0	0	3.7	0	.7	0	0	14.8	15	6.1
B. Director of extension..............	0	11.8	7.4	9	8.7	0	1.5	7.4	0	2.0
C. President.......	36.3	33.8	29.6	36	34.1	18.2	3.7	18.5	21	11.4
8. Directing conferences with boards of education										
A. Dean of the college..............	4.5	0	0	0	.7	4.5	2.9	3.7	9	4.8
B. Director of extension..............	0	0	11.1	3	2.8	0	4.4	0	6	4.1
C. Director of training................	0	1.5	3.7	3	2.0	0	2.9	3.7	6	3.4
D. President.......	36.3	38.2	14.8	33	32.8	9.1	19.1	11.1	12	14.8
E. Standing committee................	0	1.5	3.7	0	1.4	0	1.5	0	0	.7

TABLE XXVIII—*(Continued)*

Functions and Chief Administrative Officers and Groups Who Usually Perform Them	Percentage of Colleges in Which One Officer or Group Usually Performs the Administrative Function					Percentage of Colleges in Which Two or More Officers or Groups Usually Cooperate in Performing the Function				
	Enrollment					Enrollment				
	Under 300	300 to 799	800 to 1199	1200 or More	All Colleges Combined	Under 300	300 to 799	800 to 1199	1200 or More	All Colleges Combined
9. Arranging for student organizations to give community programs such as plays, concerts, etc.										
A. Dean of the college..............	0	1.5	0	0	.7	0	5.9	0	6	4.1
B. Director of extension..............	0	0	11.1	3	2.8	0	5.9	0	3	3.4
C. Head of department.............	0	10.3	11.1	9	8.7	0	8.8	7.4	12	8.1
D. President.......	31.8	11.8	14.8	9	14.8	27.2	23.5	14.8	12	20.0
E. Standing committee..............	9.1	16.7	25.9	12	16.1	13.6	8.8	3.7	15	10.0
10. Arranging for staff members to judge debates, oratorical contests, etc.										
A. Dean of the college..............	9.1	2.9	3.7	0	3.4	4.5	7.5	7.4	21	10.0
B. Director of extension..............	0	1.5	18.5	9	6.1	0	1.5	0	6	2.0
C. President.......	41.0	32.3	22.2	12	28.1	13.6	11.8	18.5	21	15.4
D. Standing committee..............	0	4.4	14.8	9	6.7	0	2.9	3.7	0	2.0

This table should be read as follows: Full responsibility for formulating policies concerning public relations is delegated to the dean of the college by none of the colleges enrolling fewer than 300 students; by none of the colleges enrolling 300–799; by none of the colleges enrolling 800–1199; and by none of the colleges enrolling 1200 or more students. In cooperation with other officers this responsibility is delegated to the dean of the college by 4.5% of the colleges enrolling under 300, etc.

Consult page 89 for a statement concerning the interpretation of the data in this table.

PUBLICITY AND PUBLICATIONS

A study of Table XXIX, page 130, shows that the presidents of teachers colleges depend to a large extent upon the registrar, the editor of publications, and standing committees to perform functions regarding publicity and publications. However, many presidents retain these functions as a part of their official duties. The presidents usually formulate and approve policies concerning publicity and publications in institutions of all sizes.

TABLE XXIX

PUBLICITY AND PUBLICATIONS

THE PERFORMANCE OF ADMINISTRATIVE FUNCTIONS IN 22 SMALL, 68 MEDIUM SIZED, 27 LARGE, AND 33 EXTRA LARGE TEACHERS COLLEGES. 1932

Functions and Chief Administrative Officers and Groups Who Usually Perform Them	Percentage of Colleges in Which One Officer or Group Usually Performs the Administrative Function					Percentage of Colleges in Which Two or More Officers or Groups Usually Cooperate in Performing the Function				
	Enrollment					Enrollment				
	Under 300	300 to 799	800 to 1199	1200 or More	All Colleges Combined	Under 300	300 to 799	800 to 1199	1200 or More	All Colleges Combined
1. Formulating policies concerning publicity and public relations										
A. Dean of the college	0	0	0	0	0	13.6	4.4	11.1	0	6.1
B. Director of extension	0	0	0	0	0	0	2.9	7.4	0	2.8
C. Editor of publications	0	5.9	7.4	9	6.1	0	13.2	7.4	18	11.4
D. President	41.0	22.1	14.8	12	21.4	31.8	42.6	37.0	36	38.7
E. Standing committee	9.1	13.2	18.5	15	14.1	13.6	16.7	3.7	18	14.1
2. Approving policies concerning publicity and public relations										
A. Dean of the college	0	0	0	0	0	4.5	1.5	7.4	3	3.4
B. President	50.0	58.8	55.5	63	58.1	22.7	25.0	22.2	18	22.8
C. State board	9.1	1.5	7.4	3	4.1	9.1	5.9	0	0	4.1
3. Directing the preparation of the college catalog										
A. Dean of the college	9.1	11.8	29.6	18	16.1	9.1	7.5	18.5	12	10.7
B. President	36.3	25.0	18.5	0	20.0	36.3	17.6	25.9	21	22.8
C. Registrar	4.5	7.5	3.7	18	8.7	4.5	13.2	22.2	12	13.4
D. Standing committee	4.5	5.9	11.1	9	7.4	9.1	11.8	11.1	15	12.0
4. Maintaining informational service										
A. Dean of the college	0	2.9	3.7	0	2.0	9.1	2.9	3.7	6	4.8
B. Director of extension	4.5	2.9	11.1	0	4.1	0	2.9	3.7	6	3.4
C. President	22.7	16.7	11.1	9	14.8	31.8	16.7	3.7	15	16.1
D. Registrar	22.7	11.8	17.5	9	14.1	22.7	8.8	3.7	9	10.0
5. Editing and publishing institutional bulletins										
A. Dean of the college	4.5	4.4	18.5	3	6.7	9.1	11.8	7.4	6	9.4

TABLE XXIX—*(Continued)*

Functions and Chief Administrative Officers and Groups Who Usually Perform Them	Percentage of Colleges in Which One Officer or Group Usually Performs the Administrative Function					Percentage of Colleges in Which Two or More Officers or Groups Usually Cooperate in Performing the Function				
	Enrollment					Enrollment				
	Under 300	300 to 799	800 to 1199	1200 or More	All Colleges Combined	Under 300	300 to 799	800 to 1199	1200 or More	All Colleges Combined
5. *(Cont'd.)*										
B. Editor of publications..............	0	8.8	11.1	13	8.7	0	5.9	3.7	9	5.4
C. President.......	18.2	7.5	7.4	3	8.1	45.4	27.9	22.2	15	26.7
D. Registrar.......	4.5	4.4	3.7	6	4.8	13.6	7.5	25.9	6	11.4
E. Standing committee...............	4.5	13.2	7.4	18	12.0	45.0	11.8	3.7	18	10.7
6. Furnishing news stories to the press										
A. Dean of the college..............	4.5	1.5	3.7	0	2.0	9.1	1.5	3.7	6	4.1
B. Director of extension...............	0	1.5	3.7	0	1.4	4.5	0	3.7	0	1.4
C. Editor of publications..............	4.5	16.7	18.5	24	16.7	0	5.9	0	15	6.1
D. President.......	22.7	11.8	22.2	9	14.8	31.8	32.1	11.1	15	20.0
E. Standing committee...............	4.5	17.6	3.7	15	12.8	4.5	8.8	7.4	3	6.7
7. Distributing information concerning campus courses										
A. Dean of the college..............	9.1	8.8	3.7	3	6.7	13.6	8.8	3.7	6	8.1
B. Director of extension...............	0	1.5	14.8	9	5.4	4.5	5.9	3.7	3	4.8
C. Editor of publications..............	0	8.8	3.7	9	6.7	0	2.9	0	12	4.1
D. President.......	22.7	8.8	11.1	0	9.4	27.2	27.9	3.7	15	21.4
E. Registrar.......	9.1	13.2	44.4	27	21.4	41.0	14.7	0	12	15.4
8. Distributing information concerning extension courses										
A. Dean of the college..............	4.5	7.5	0	0	4.1	0	1.5	14.8	0	3.4
B. Director of extension...............	9.1	14.7	14.8	42	20.0	0	5.9	3.7	12	6.1
C. Editor of publications..............	0	1.5	7.4	0	2.0	0	4.4	0	3	2.8
D. President.......	9.1	2.9	11.1	9	6.7	13.6	7.5	3.7	6	7.4
E. Registrar.......	13.6	2.9	18.5	9	8.7	9.1	2.9	11.1	9	6.7
9. Establishing friendly relations with the press										
A. Dean of the college..............	4.5	0	0	3	1.4	13.6	4.4	7.4	3	6.1

TABLE XXIX—*(Continued)*

Functions and Chief Administrative Officers and Groups Who Usually Perform Them	Percentage of Colleges in Which One Officer or Group Usually Performs the Administrative Function					Percentage of Colleges in Which Two or More Officers or Groups Usually Cooperate in Performing the Function				
	Enrollment					Enrollment				
	Under 300	300 to 799	800 to 1199	1200 or More	All Colleges Combined	Under 300	300 to 799	800 to 1199	1200 or More	All Colleges Combined
9. (Cont'd.)										
B. Director of extension...............	0	1.5	22.2	3	5.4	4.5	2.9	3.7	3	3.4
C. Editor of publications..............	0	8.8	11.1	18	10.0	4.5	7.5	0	15	7.4
D. President.......	31.8	22.1	18.5	24	23.4	41.0	20.6	11.1	15	20.7
E. Standing committee................	0	4.4	3.7	9	4.8	0	10.3	3.7	3	6.1
10. Determining news values										
A. Dean of the college...............	4.5	1.5	3.7	0	2.0	4.5	0	7.4	0	2.0
B. Editor of publications..............	4.5	8.8	18.5	21	12.8	4.5	10.3	0	15	8.7
C. President.......	22.7	17.6	29.6	21	21.4	36.3	13.2	11.1	9	15.4
D. Standing committee................	4.5	14.7	0	6	8.7	0	5.9	0	3	3.4
11. Advertising										
A. Business manager	4.5	1.5	7.4	9	4.8	9.1	1.5	3.7	3	3.4
B. Editor of publications..............	4.5	8.8	3.7	9	7.4	4.5	2.9	3.7	6	4.1
C. President.......	27.2	22.1	25.9	21	23.4	27.2	8.8	14.8	9	12.8
D. Standing committee................	4.5	4.4	3.7	3	4.1	0	4.4	0	3	2.8
12. Collection and compilation of mailing lists										
A. Dean of the college...............	0	2.9	0	0	1.4	4.5	2.9	7.4	6	4.3
B. Director of extension...............	0	2.9	3.7	6	3.4	0	2.9	11.1	9	5.4
C. President.......	4.5	11.3	25.9	6	12.0	9.1	16.7	3.7	9	11.4
D. Registrar.......	59.0	19.1	25.9	18	26.1	9.1	13.2	11.1	18	13.4

This table should be read as follows: Full responsibility for formulating policies concerning publicity and public relations is delegated to the dean of the college by none of the colleges enrolling fewer than 300 students; by none of the colleges enrolling 300–799; by none of the colleges enrolling 800–1199; and by none of the colleges enrolling 1200 or more students. In cooperation with other officers this responsibility is delegated to the dean of the college by 13.6% of the colleges enrolling under 300, etc. Consult page 89 for a statement concerning interpretation of the data in this table.

They establish friendly relations with the press and determine news values. The president prepares the college catalog and arranges for any advertising which is done. Other publicity and publications functions are usually delegated.

College deans in some institutions perform functions concerning publicity and publications. They cooperate in the formulation and approval of policies but never have full responsibility for these functions. They are called upon to direct the preparation of the college catalog more than any other subordinate official. Some few institutions depend upon their deans to edit institutional bulletins and to distribute information concerning campus courses. The deans have but a small share in other functions pertaining to publicity and publications.

Registrars are frequently responsible for publicity functions other than those connected with the daily press. They help prepare the catalog. The president is the only officer who maintains informational service in more institutions than the registrar. Information concerning campus and extension courses is frequently distributed by him. More particularly in small institutions but quite generally in all institutions, the registrar collects and compiles mailing lists.

Although there are approximately one-third of the colleges which have editors of publications, only a small percentage of them use this official in editing and publishing institutional bulletins. Half of the institutions having an editor of publications delegate to him the job of furnishing news stories to the press. In a very few institutions he distributes information about courses. There is a tendency to have the editor establish relations with the press and to determine news values. On the whole, the reports from the 150 institutions investigated do not establish the editor of publications as a dominant official in publicity and publications.

STUDENT ORGANIZATION

An analysis of Table XXX, page 134, shows that functions pertaining to student organizations are largely performed by committees and department heads. Committees dominate in the formulation of policies, with some cooperative assistance from the student council. Special and standing committees

TABLE XXX

STUDENT ORGANIZATIONS

THE PERFORMANCE OF ADMINISTRATIVE FUNCTIONS IN 22 SMALL, 68 MEDIUM SIZED, 27 LARGE, AND 33 EXTRA LARGE TEACHERS COLLEGES. 1932

Functions and Chief Administrative Officers and Groups Who Usually Perform Them	Percentage of Colleges in Which One Officer or Group Usually Performs the Administrative Function					Percentage of Colleges in Which Two or More Officers or Groups Usually Cooperate in Performing the Function				
	Enrollment					Enrollment				
	Under 300	300 to 799	800 to 1199	1200 or More	All Colleges Combined	Under 300	300 to 799	800 to 1199	1200 or More	All Colleges Combined
1. Formulating policies concerning student organizations										
A. Dean of the college	4.5	0	3.7	0	1.4	4.5	8.8	3.7	9	7.4
B. Dean of men	4.5	0	0	0	.7	4.5	19.1	11.1	27	17.4
C. Dean of women	0	0	0	0	0	31.8	36.8	14.8	33	31.4
D. Faculty council	0	2.9	3.7	0	2.0	0	5.9	3.7	6	4.8
E. President	9.1	2.9	3.7	6	4.8	45.4	35.3	14.8	27	31.4
F. Standing committee	9.1	11.8	37.0	24	18.7	36.3	23.5	22.2	21	24.8
G. Student council	9.1	1.5	11.1	6	5.4	13.6	8.8	29.6	6	12.8
2. Approving policies concerning student organizations										
A. Dean of the college	0	0	0	0	0	0	10.3	3.7	6	6.7
B. Dean of men	0	0	0	0	0	9.1	11.8	3.7	12	10.0
C. Dean of women	0	0	0	0	0	13.6	17.6	11.1	12	14.8
D. Faculty as a whole	9.6	1.5	11.1	6	5.4	9.1	8.8	3.7	12	8.7
E. President	54.5	35.3	33.3	45	40.0	22.7	33.8	33.3	21	29.4
F. Standing committee	4.5	2.9	7.4	9	5.4	4.5	14.7	7.4	3	9.4
G. Student council	0	0	0	6	1.4	9.1	4.4	7.4	6	7.4
3. Approving sponsors for organizations										
A. Dean of the college	0	1.5	0	0	.7	4.5	8.8	7.4	6	7.4
B. Dean of men	0	0	0	0	0	9.1	19.1	18.5	15	16.7
C. Dean of women	0	2.9	0	6	2.1	18.2	25.0	25.9	18	22.8
D. President	68.1	39.7	33.3	42	43.4	13.6	25.0	18.5	12	24.8
4. Granting permits for organization activities										
A. Dean of the college	0	0	3.7	0	.7	0	8.8	3.7	0	4.8
B. Dean of men	0	0	0	3	.7	13.6	17.6	18.5	24	18.7
C. Dean of women	0	5.9	0	6	4.1	31.8	29.4	25.9	24	28.1
D. President	50.0	25.0	22.2	12	25.4	27.2	19.1	18.5	15	19.1
E. Standing committee	4.5	10.3	25.9	21	14.8	4.5	2.9	7.4	6	4.8

TABLE XXX—(*Continued*)

Functions and Chief Administrative Officers and Groups Who Usually Perform Them	Percentage of Colleges in Which One Officer or Group Usually Performs the Administrative Function					Percentage of Colleges in Which Two or More Officers or Groups Usually Cooperate in Performing the Function				
	Enrollment					Enrollment				
	Under 300	300 to 799	800 to 1199	1200 or More	All Colleges Combined	Under 300	300 to 799	800 to 1199	1200 or More	All Colleges Combined
5. Directing student dramatics										
A. Head of department..............	31.8	44.4	40.7	63	46.1	4.5	2.9	3.7	0	2.8
B. Special committee	27.2	14.7	22.2	24	20.0	0	0	0	0	0
C. Standing committee...............	0	10.3	25.9	3	10.0	0	0	0	0	0
6. Directing college debating										
A. Head of department..............	22.7	36.8	29.6	51	36.7	0	1.5	3.7	0	1.4
B. Special committee	18.2	11.8	18.5	15	14.8	0	0	0	0	0
C. Standing committee...............	4.5	14.7	29.6	15	16.1	0	0	0	0	0
7. Directing student publications										
A. Editor of publications..............	13.6	13.2	7.4	15	12.8	4.5	1.5	0	6	2.8
B. Head of department..............	22.7	14.7	22.2	9	16.1	4.5	2.9	0	3	2.8
C. Special committee	22.7	8.8	14.8	33	17.4	0	0	3.7	0	.7
D. Standing committee...............	4.5	25.0	29.6	18	21.4	0	5.9	3.7	3	4.1
8. Directing college athletics										
A. Director of athletics..............	45.4	36.9	33.3	54	41.4	13.6	13.2	14.8	6	12.0
B. Head of department..............	13.6	16.7	11.1	6	12.8	4.5	4.4	3.7	0	3.4
C. Special committee	9.1	2.9	3.7	6	4.8	4.5	2.9	3.7	0	2.8
D. Standing committee...............	4.5	13.2	37.0	18	17.4	4.5	7.5	7.4	6	6.7

This table should be read as follows: Full responsibility for formulating policies concerning student organizations is delegated to the dean of the college by 4.5% of the colleges enrolling fewer than 300 students; by none of the colleges enrolling 300–799; by 3.7% of the colleges enrolling 800–1199; and by none of the colleges enrolling 1200 or more students. In cooperation with other officers this responsibility is delegated to the dean of the college by 4.5% of the colleges enrolling under 300, etc.
Consult page 89 for a statement concerning interpretation of data in this table.

grant permits for organization activities, especially in the larger institutions.   Student dramatics, college debating, and student publications are directed by committees more frequently than by individuals.   There is, however, a fairly large percentage of institutions which centralize these activities under the direction of heads of departments.   It seems reasonable to assume that dramatics, debating, and publications are a part of, or at least closely allied to, the department of English.   The centering of responsibility for the performance of these functions with the head of the English department is in accord with the criterion which states related functions should be grouped under the direction or control of an officer who in turn is responsible to the president.

College athletics are under the direction of the department of athletics in more than half of the institutions investigated. This is true for institutions of all sizes.   This statement is based on the data reported in Table XII, page 63, which shows that directors of athletics are, for the majority of institutions, also heads of the departments of physical education.   Table XXX shows that directors of athletics and heads of physical education departments are responsible for the athletic program in 54 per cent of the colleges.   Administrative officers other than department heads have responsibility in but few institutions concerning student organizations.   The dean of the college, in approximately 7 per cent of the institutions, cooperates in formulating policies, in approving policies and sponsors, and in granting permits for organization activities.   The deans of men and deans of women cooperate in these same functions in a larger percentage of the institutions than the college deans, but on the average their cooperation is limited to approximately 20 per cent of the institutions investigated.   These data indicate that functions pertaining to student organization are on the whole administered by groups and not by individuals.

STUDENT SOCIAL ACTIVITIES

An examination of Table XXXI, page 137, shows that teachers colleges of all sizes use committees more frequently than administrative officers in performing the duties involved in the direction and control of student activities.   Committees

TABLE XXXI

STUDENT SOCIAL ACTIVITIES

THE PERFORMANCE OF ADMINISTRATIVE FUNCTIONS IN 22 SMALL, 68 MEDIUM SIZED, 27 LARGE, AND 33 EXTRA LARGE TEACHERS COLLEGES. 1932

Functions and Chief Administrative Officers and Groups Who Usually Perform Them	Percentage of Colleges in Which One Officer or Group Usually Performs the Administrative Function					Percentage of Colleges in Which Two or More Officers or Groups Usually Cooperate in Performing the Function				
	Enrollment					Enrollment				
	Under 300	300 to 799	800 to 1199	1200 or More	All Colleges Combined	Under 300	300 to 799	800 to 1199	1200 or More	All Colleges Combined
1. Formulating policies concerning student social activities										
A. Dean of men....	0	0	0	0	0	27.2	23.5	14.8	33	24.8
B. Dean of women..	0	11.8	3.7	12	8.7	41.0	35.3	37.0	39	37.4
C. Dir. social affairs	0	4.4	3.7	9	4.8	0	4.4	0	6	3.4
D. President.......	4.5	1.5	0	0	1.4	36.3	11.8	7.4	6	13.4
E. Standing committee...............	22.7	17.6	18.5	27	20.7	27.2	17.6	14.8	21	19.4
F. Student council..	4.5	4.4	11.1	3	5.4	22.7	10.3	7.4	6	10.7
2. Approving policies concerning student social activities										
A. Dean of the college...............	0	1.5	0	0	.7	0	2.9	7.4	6	4.1
B. Dean of men....	0	0	0	0	0	13.6	16.7	11.1	18	15.4
C. Dean of women..	0	7.5	3.7	0	4.1	18.2	29.4	25.9	24	26.1
D. Faculty council..	4.5	0	3.7	0	1.4	4.5	4.4	3.7	6	4.8
E. President.......	54.5	29.4	22.2	36	33.4	18.2	20.6	22.2	27	22.0
F. Standing committee...............	13.6	4.4	11.1	12	8.7	4.5	11.8	3.7	24	12.0
G. Student council..	0	0	3.7	3	1.4	4.5	7.5	0	6	5.4
3. Planning social activities for student groups										
A. Dean of the college...............	0	0	0	0	0	0	4.4	3.7	0	2.8
B. Dean of men....	0	0	0	0	0	13.6	25.0	18.5	30	23.4
C. Dean of women..	4.5	8.8	7.4	9	8.1	31.8	39.7	29.6	36	36.1
D. Director of student social affairs...	4.5	4.4	7.4	6	5.4	0	5.9	3.7	9	5.4
E. President.......	4.5	2.9	0	0	2.0	9.1	4.4	3.7	9	6.1
F. Standing committee...............	27.2	20.6	11.1	18	19.4	13.6	29.4	14.8	33	25.4
G. Student council..	9.1	2.9	7.4	6	5.4	22.7	19.1	14.8	12	17.4
4. Supervising general conduct at social affairs										
A. Dean of the college...............	0	0	0	0	0	0	4.4	7.4	3	4.1

TABLE XXXI—(*Continued*)

Functions and Chief Administrative Officers and Groups Who Usually Perform Them	Percentage of Colleges in Which One Officer or Group Usually Performs the Administrative Function					Percentage of Colleges in Which Two or More Officers or Groups Usually Cooperate in Performing the Function				
	Enrollment					Enrollment				
	Under 300	300 to 799	800 to 1199	1200 or More	All Colleges Combined	Under 300	300 to 799	800 to 1199	1200 or More	All Colleges Combined
4. (*Cont'd.*)										
B. Dean of men....	1.0	1.5	0	0	.7	27.2	27.9	25.9	42	30.7
C. Dean of women..	13.6	16.7	14.8	9	14.1	41.0	39.7	33.3	48	40.7
D. Director of student social affairs...	0	1.5	7.4	9	4.1	4.5	7.5	3.7	6	6.1
E. Special committee	13.6	7.5	7.4	0	6.7	9.1	10.3	7.4	9	9.4
F. Standing committee................	9.1	7.5	11.1	12	9.4	18.2	10.3	7.4	15	12.0
G. Student council..	4.5	1.5	3.7	6	3.4	9.1	13.2	3.7	3	8.7
5. Keeping the calendar for social events										
A. Dean of men....	0	1.5	0	6	2.0	13.6	11.8	7.4	12	11.4
B. Dean of women..	22.7	27.9	25.9	33	28.1	18.2	14.7	7.4	15	14.1
C. Director of social activities..........	1.0	1.5	7.4	12	4.8	0	4.4	3.7	3	3.4
D. President.......	9.1	5.9	3.7	3	5.4	13.6	4.4	3.7	3	5.4
E. Special committee	9.1	5.9	0	3	4.8	4.5	1.5	0	3	2.0
F. Standing committee................	9.1	7.5	25.9	9	11.4	4.5	4.4	3.7	3	4.1
6. Granting permits to use college buildings for social affairs										
A. Dean of men....	4.5	0	0	3	1.4	9.1	5.9	18.5	15	11.4
B. Dean of women..	0	7.5	3.7	12	6.7	9.1	11.8	25.9	3	12.0
C. President.......	68.1	36.8	33.3	12	35.4	13.6	13.2	22.2	21	16.7
D. Standing committee................	0	10.3	7.4	6	7.4	0	7.4	3.7	3	4.8

This table should be read as follows: Full responsibility for formulating policies concerning student social activities is delegated to the dean of men in none of the colleges. In cooperation with other officers this responsibility is delegated to the dean of men in 27.2% of the colleges enrolling fewer than 300 students, in 23.5% of the colleges enrolling 300 to 799 students, etc.

Consult page 89 for a statement concerning the interpretation of the data in this table.

formulate policies, plan the social activities, and supervise general conduct at social affairs more frequently than do administrative officers. Although the presidents usually approve policies concerning student social activities, some institutional heads have delegated this function to committees. The dean of women is the officer who usually keeps the calendar for social events. But even this function is performed by a standing or special committee in approximately one college in six.

The presidents usually retain control of the use of buildings by students.   In a few cases this function is delegated to the dean of men, the dean of women, or a standing committee. However, more than half of the presidents retain this function for which they hold themselves fully or partially responsible. Since nearly all social events require the use of a building, it is reasonable to assume that all plans for social activities must await, to a large measure, the permit for the use of the building. If the president is out of the city or occupied with other administrative duties, it seems likely that those individuals working on student social affairs will be delayed in getting the president's approval to use buildings.   Delays dissipate both energy and morale.   Hence it seems that those presidents who delegate to subordinate officials the authority to grant permits for the use of buildings are relieving themselves of a routine function and saving themselves time to use in formulating administrative and instructional policies and at the same time are making for greater efficiency.

A small percentage of the colleges in this study reports that a large share of the administration of student social activities has been delegated to the student council.   Some colleges depend upon the students through their council to formulate and approve policies.   Other institutions have delegated the planning of social activities and the supervision of social affairs to the student council, with the deans of men and deans of women responsible for general oversight and management.

STUDENT STANDARDS OF CONDUCT

An examination of Table XXXII, page 140, shows several practices which predominate in the performance of functions regarding student standards of conduct.   The presidents usually delegate all functions in this group except the approving of policies.   For this function they retain the responsibility either alone or in cooperation with subordinate officers or groups in approximately two-thirds of the institutions.   All other functions are performed more frequently by subordinate officers than by the presidents.

A striking fact concerning the college deans is shown in Table XXXII.   None of the duties involved in the functions pertain-

TABLE XXXII

STUDENT STANDARDS OF CONDUCT

THE PERFORMANCE OF ADMINISTRATIVE FUNCTIONS IN 22 SMALL, 68 MEDIUM SIZED, 27 LARGE, AND 33 EXTRA LARGE TEACHERS COLLEGES. 1932

Functions and Chief Administrative Officers and Groups Who Usually Perform Them	Percentage of Colleges in Which One Officer or Group Usually Performs the Administrative Function					Percentage of Colleges in Which Two or More Officers or Groups Usually Cooperate in Performing the Function				
	Enrollment					Enrollment				
	Under 300	300 to 799	800 to 1199	1200 or More	All Colleges Combined	Under 300	300 to 799	800 to 1199	1200 or More	All Colleges Combined
1. Formulating policies concerning student standards of conduct										
A. Dean of the college	0	0	0	0	0	4.5	4.4	14.8	12	8.1
B. Dean of men	0	0	0	0	0	22.7	27.9	55.5	39	34.8
C. Dean of women	9.1	0	0	0	1.4	41.0	47.0	66.6	42	48.7
D. Faculty as a whole	13.6	2.9	7.4	3	5.4	13.6	13.2	18.5	9	13.4
E. President	4.5	1.5	10.0	3	2.0	27.2	25.0	18.5	36	26.7
F. Special committee	0	5.9	3.7	3	4.1	9.1	4.4	0	3	4.1
G. Standing committee	4.5	7.5	14.8	3	7.4	13.6	13.2	7.4	33	16.7
H. Student council	9.1	4.4	7.4	6	6.1	36.3	26.5	14.8	18	24.1
2. Approving policies concerning student standards of conduct										
A. Dean of the college	0	0	0	0	0	0	5.9	3.7	9	6.1
B. Dean of men	0	0	0	0	0	9.1	20.6	33.3	24	22.0
C. Dean of women	0	1.5	3.7	0	1.4	13.6	33.8	48.1	24	31.4
D. President	59.0	23.5	33.3	36	33.4	18.2	39.7	48.1	33	36.7
E. Standing committee	4.5	4.4	3.7	0	3.4	4.5	2.9	7.4	18	7.4
F. Student council	4.5	0	3.7	0	1.4	4.5	11.8	3.7	6	8.1
3. Investigating reported offenses										
A. Dean of the college	0	0	0	0	0	9.1	11.8	11.1	18	12.8
B. Dean of men	0	0	0	0	0	18.2	36.8	51.8	60	42.0
C. Dean of women	9.1	1.5	3.7	0	2.8	36.3	45.6	62.9	63	51.4
D. President	4.5	5.9	7.4	0	4.8	50.0	20.6	18.5	21	24.8
E. Special committee	4.5	5.9	3.7	3	4.8	4.5	5.9	3.7	3	4.8
F. Standing committee	13.6	4.4	22.2	12	10.7	9.1	11.8	3.7	6	8.7
G. Student council	4.5	5.9	7.4	0	4.8	27.2	17.6	7.4	6	14.8
4. Building attitudes of right conduct										
A. Dean of the college	0	0	0	0	0	0	10.3	11.1	9	8.7
B. Dean of men	0	0	0	3	.7	22.7	26.5	48.1	33	31.4

TABLE XXXII—(*Continued*)

Functions and Chief Administrative Officers and Groups Who Usually Perform Them	Percentage of Colleges in Which One Officer or Group Usually Performs the Administrative Function					Percentage of Colleges in Which Two or More Officers or Groups Usually Cooperate in Performing the Function				
	Enrollment					Enrollment				
	Under 300	300 to 799	800 to 1199	1200 or More	All Colleges Combined	Under 300	300 to 799	800 to 1199	1200 or More	All Colleges Combined
4. (*Cont'd.*)										
C. Dean of women..	9.1	1.5	3.7	0	2.8	36.3	33.8	62.9	36	40.0
D. Faculty as a whole	9.1	20.6	25.9	15	18.7	36.3	17.6	11.1	15	18.7
E. President.......	0	1.5	3.7	0	1.4	41.0	23.5	14.8	18	23.4
F. Standing committee...............	9.1	5.9	7.4	9	7.4	4.5	11.8	0	6	7.4
G. Student council..	9.1	2.9	3.7	3	4.1	36.3	20.6	14.8	3	18.1
5. Punishing violators of conduct standards										
A. Dean of the college...............	0	1.5	0	0	.7	0	7.5	7.4	15	8.1
B. Dean of men....	0	0	0	0	0	4.5	26.5	40.7	36	28.1
C. Dean of women..	0	0	0	0	0	27.2	30.9	51.8	33	34.8
D. President.......	31.8	14.7	11.1	9	15.4	36.3	41.2	22.2	39	36.7
E. Standing committee...............	9.1	10.3	18.5	21	14.1	9.1	16.7	7.4	21	14.8
F. Student council..	9.1	5.9	11.1	0	6.1	27.2	19.1	18.5	9	18.1
6. Controlling and supervising students outside of class										
A. Dean of the college...............	0	0	0	0	0	0	7.5	11.1	18	9.4
B. Dean of men....	4.5	0	0	3	1.4	36.3	32.3	59.2	51	42.0
C. Dean of women..	13.6	0	0	3	2.8	54.5	42.6	70.3	51	44.8
D. Faculty as a whole	4.5	2.9	0	3	2.8	18.2	5.9	0	3	6.1
E. President.......	4.5	4.4	3.7	0	3.4	31.8	70.6	14.8	18	43.4
F. Standing committee...............	0	8.8	3.7	9	6.7	9.1	10.3	3.7	9	8.7
G. Student council..	0	8.8	11.1	0	6.1	31.8	13.2	14.8	0	13.4

This table should be read as follows: Full responsibility for formulating policies concerning student standards of conduct is delegated to the dean of the college by none of the colleges enrolling fewer than 300 students; by none of the colleges enrolling 300–799; by none of the colleges enrolling 800–1199; and by none of the colleges enrolling 1200 or more students. In cooperation with other officers this responsibility is delegated to the dean of the college by 4.5% of the colleges enrolling under 300, etc. Consult page 89 for a statement concerning the interpretation of the data in this table.

ing to student standards of conduct is reported as performed by the college dean except in cooperation with other officers. Approximately 10 per cent of the college deans cooperate in the performance of these functions but none performs them alone. This cooperative responsibility is found more frequently in

larger colleges.   Deans of women perform functions in some
institutions where apparently the deans of men have no responsibility.   The function which concerns the investigation of
reported offenses illustrates this relationship.   In a few colleges
of all sizes, the dean of women is alone responsible for investigating reported offenses.   None of the deans of men has this
responsibility except in cooperation with other officials.   No
institutions report either the dean of men or the dean of women
as alone responsible for punishing violators of conduct standards.   This responsibility when not retained by the president
is delegated either to a committee or to two or more officials.

The student council in some institutions enters into all functions pertaining to standards of conduct.   In approximately
30 per cent of the colleges the student council has a voice in
formulating policies relative to conduct standards.   In some
institutions policies are approved by the student council.   It
investigates reported offenses, cooperates in the building of
right attitudes, punishes violators of conduct standards, and
helps control and supervise students outside of class.

STUDENT–TEACHING

An analysis of Table XXXIII, page 143, shows that one
officer, the director of training, is dominantly in control of
student-teaching in all the 150 colleges investigated.   This is
true regardless of the size of the institution.   He is assisted in
nearly all functions by the elementary and high school principals.   He is the chief officer in formulating policies and has
much to do with their approval.   Equipment for the training
school is planned chiefly by him.   The training school curricula are principally his responsibility.   In institutions of all
sizes he assigns the student-teachers and supervises them in
their practice teaching in both the elementary and high schools.
He cooperates in rating their work, although but few directors
have full responsibility in rating.

Department heads have only a small share of responsibility in
student-teaching.   They share in one out of four institutions in
formulating policies.   They do not plan training school equipment nor help to any extent in the construction or revision of
the training school curricula.   A small percentage of them

TABLE XXXIII

STUDENT–TEACHING

THE PERFORMANCE OF ADMINISTRATIVE FUNCTIONS IN 22 SMALL, 68 MEDIUM SIZED, 27 LARGE, AND 33 EXTRA LARGE TEACHERS COLLEGES. 1932

Functions and Chief Administrative Officers and Groups Who Usually Perform Them	Percentage of Colleges in Which One Officer or Group Usually Performs the Administrative Function					Percentage of Colleges in Which Two or More Officers or Groups Usually Cooperate in Performing the Function				
	Enrollment					Enrollment				
	Under 300	300 to 799	800 to 1199	1200 or More	All Colleges Combined	Under 300	300 to 799	800 to 1199	1200 or More	All Colleges Combined
1. Formulating policies concerning student-teaching										
A. Dean of the college...............	0	2.9	0	0	1.4	18.2	8.8	25.5	18	22.0
B. Director of training................	13.6	25.0	29.6	39	27.4	72.6	45.6	48.1	51	51.4
C. El. school principal................	4.5	0	0	0	.7	4.5	10.3	14.8	6	9.4
D. Head of department...............	0	1.5	0	0	.7	0	17.6	11.1	6	11.4
E. High school principal...............	0	0	0	0	0	0	4.4	7.4	6	4.8
F. President.......	4.5	4.4	0	0	2.8	41.0	26.5	18.5	21	26.1
G. Training staff....	4.5	0	7.4	0	2.0	13.6	5.9	11.1	9	8.7
2. Approving policies concerning student-teaching										
A. Dean of the college.............	0	2.9	7.4	3	3.4	4.5	8.8	18.5	6	8.7
B. Director of training................	0	10.3	14.8	12	10.0	27.2	27.9	25.9	27	27.4
C. Faculty as a whole	4.5	1.5	0	9	3.4	13.6	4.4	0	6	5.4
D. President.......	68.1	26.5	25.9	33	34.1	22.7	35.3	25.9	21	28.7
E. Special committee	0	0	7.4	0	1.4	0	11.8	7.4	9	8.7
F. State board.....	4.5	2.9	0	0	2.0	4.5	2.9	1	3	2.8
3. Planning equipment for training school										
A. Director of training................	22.7	25.0	33.3	45	30.7	86.3	50.0	44.4	39	52.0
B. El. school principal................	0	0	3.7	0	.7	18.2	11.8	7.4	9	11.4
C. High school principal...............	0	0	0	0	0	4.5	2.9	7.4	6	4.8
D. President.......	13.6	2.9	0	3	4.1	54.5	32.3	29.6	21	32.8
E. Training staff...	4.5	1.5	7.4	3	3.4	27.2	8.8	14.8	9	12.8

TABLE XXXIII—(*Continued*)

Functions and Chief Administrative Officers and Groups Who Usually Perform Them	Percentage of Colleges in Which One Officer or Group Usually Performs the Administrative Function					Percentage of Colleges in Which Two or More Officers or Groups Usually Cooperate in Performing the Function				
	Enrollment					Enrollment				
	Under 300	300 to 799	800 to 1199	1200 or More	All Colleges Combined	Under 300	300 to 799	800 to 1199	1200 or More	All Colleges Combined
4. Construction and revision of training school curricula										
A. Dean of the college..............	0	1.5	0	0	.7	0	5.9	7.4	6	5.4
B. Director of training................	27.2	26.5	18.5	12	22.0	50.0	41.2	44.4	63	48.1
C. El. school principal.................	0	0	0	3	.7	13.6	10.3	14.8	12	12.0
D. High school principal...............	0	0	0	3	.7	0	8.6	22.2	9	10.0
E. President.......	4.5	0	0	0	.7	41.0	10.3	7.4	21	16.7
F. Training staff...	4.5	1.5	11.1	6	4.8	27.2	19.1	22.2	24	22.0
G. State board.....	0	4.4	11.1	0	4.1	0	4.4	0	0	2.0
5. Selecting and assigning student-teachers in the elementary school										
A. Dean of the college..............	0	2.9	0	0	1.4	4.5	5.9	11.1	6	6.7
B. Director of training................	50.0	51.5	40.7	54	50.0	31.8	23.5	44.4	33	30.7
C. El. school principal.................	0	1.5	7.4	3	2.8	18.2	7.5	11.1	12	10.7
D. President.......	9.1	0	0	0	1.4	18.2	2.9	3.7	3	5.4
E. Training staff...	4.5	1.5	3.7	0	2.0	4.5	4.4	14.8	6	6.7
6. Selecting and assigning student-teachers in the college high school										
A. Dean of the college..............	0	0	0	0	0	0	4.4	14.8	6	6.1
B. Director of training................	22.7	25.0	22.2	45	28.7	31.8	23.5	44.4	21	28.1
C. Head of department..............	0	2.9	3.7	0	2.0	0	5.9	7.4	6	5.4
D. High school principal...............	4.5	2.9	11.1	6	5.4	0	7.5	7.4	9	6.7
E. President.......	4.5	0	0	0	.7	4.5	2.9	0	3	2.0
7. Supervising student-teachers in the elementary school										
A. Director of training................	36.3	32.3	25.9	33	32.0	41.0	26.5	22.2	27	28.1
B. El. school principal.................	0	4.4	7.4	9	5.4	18.2	10.3	3.7	12	10.7

TABLE XXXIII—(*Continued*)

Functions and Chief Administrative Officers and Groups Who Usually Perform Them	Percentage of Colleges in Which One Officer or Group Usually Performs the Administrative Function					Percentage of Colleges in Which Two or More Officers or Groups Usually Cooperate in Performing the Function				
	Enrollment					Enrollment				
	Under 300	300 to 799	800 to 1199	1200 or More	All Colleges Combined	Under 300	300 to 799	800 to 1199	1200 or More	All Colleges Combined
7. (*Cont.²*)										
C. Head of department...............	4.5	5.9	3.7	3	4.8	4.5	2.9	3.7	3	3.4
D. Training staff....	4.5	10.3	40.7	6	14.1	9.1	20.6	14.8	24	18.7
8. Supervising student-teachers in the college high school										
A. Director of training...............	22.7	16.7	14.8	18	17.4	9.1	19.1	29.6	27	21.4
B. Head of department...............	4.5	5.9	3.7	3	4.8	4.5	4.4	11.1	0	4.8
C. High school principal...............	4.5	2.9	3.7	9	4.8	4.5	7.5	0	9	6.1
D. Training staff...	4.5	8.8	22.2	3	9.4	9.1	8.8	29.6	27	16.7
9. Rating student-teachers										
A. Director of training...............	22.7	13.2	14.8	12	14.8	50.0	41.2	48.1	39	44.1
B. El. school principal...............	4.5	0	0	3	1.4	9.1	13.2	14.8	24	15.4
C. Head of department...............	0	4.4	0	0	2.0	9.1	10.3	7.4	3	8.1
D. High school principal...............	4.5	0	0	0	.7	4.5	5.9	3.7	15	7.4
E. President.......	0	0	0	0	0	22.7	1.5	0	0	4.1
F. Training staff....	9.1	16.7	25.9	12	16.1	31.8	27.9	33.3	45	32.0

This table should be read as follows: Full responsibility for formulating policies concerning student-teaching is delegated to the dean of the college by none of the colleges enrolling fewer than 300 students; by 2.9% of the colleges enrolling 300–799; by none of the colleges enrolling 800–1199; and by none of the colleges enrolling 1200 or more students. In cooperation with other officers this responsibility is delegated to the dean of the college by 18.2% of the colleges enrolling under 300, etc.
Consult page 89 for a statement concerning the interpretation of the data in this table.

helps in the assignment of teachers in the high school, but none has this responsibility in the elementary school. Probably the heads of departments have little to do with the assignment of teachers in the elementary school because they may consider the elementary teaching as outside of their departments. A surprisingly small percentage of department heads supervise their students in either the elementary or high school, and only about 10 per cent of the institutions delegate any responsibility concerning rating of student-teaching to heads of departments. These data indicate that student-teaching for the most part is not integrated with the subject matter departments.

Other dominant facts are shown by the data in Table XXX-III.   A comparison of the tables in this chapter shows that the presidents delegate functions of student-teaching more completely than other functions in administration.   The president approves the policies, but beyond that he enters but little into student-teaching.   Other administrative officers than the directors of training have little responsibility pertaining to student-teaching.   The dean cooperates in the performance of a few functions but has little direct responsibility.   Other officers, such as the dean of men, dean of women, and director of placement, are practically out of the student-teaching picture.   The state board in a few institutions approves policies and helps in the construction and revision of the training school curricula.   However, on the whole, the state board retains very little responsibility for student-teaching.   In some institutions the faculty as a whole does approve policies, but in the large, student-teaching seems isolated.   If student-teaching is the heart of the teacher-training program it seems reasonable to expect a larger participation by administrative officials in formulating policies concerning student-teaching than is revealed by the data.

STUDENT WELFARE

A study of Table XXXIV, page 148, shows that, with the exception of the approval of policies, those administrative functions which pertain to student welfare are delegated rather than retained by nearly all teachers college presidents.   Very few presidents depend upon any one single individual to formulate policies.   Standing committees are used more than any other agency.   The deans of men and deans of women cooperate in the formulation of policies, but they are not individually responsible for policy formulation.   The director of health cooperates in a few of the larger institutions.   Since health and welfare are so closely interrelated, it seems that more presidents should use their directors of health service in formulating welfare policies.   Table VI, page 52, shows that 63.4 per cent of the institutions have directors of health service and yet, as indicated in Table XXXIV, page 148, only 6.7 per cent of them help in formulating welfare policies. It seems reasonable to believe that standards for rooms, conditions under which students work, and even the entertainment features, such as excursions, picnics, and the like, are all factors closely related to health and hence natural functions for the concern and attention of directors of health service.

Other functions concerning the welfare of students are distributed among different officers. The deans of men and the deans of women cooperate in providing a list of suitable rooms for students. Comments made by presidents in their original reports indicate that the deans of men and deans of women perform similar functions regarding the inspection and approval of rooms, the one officer limiting his efforts to rooms for men, the other restricting her activities to rooms for women. Supervision of student health service is centered under the control of the directors of health service with cooperative assistance from deans of men and deans of women. A standing committee is the agency most frequently used to help students find part-time employment. Deans of men and deans of women cooperate in helping students find part-time employment. Placing the functions of student employment in the hands of one individual, such as the dean of women or the dean of men, is in line with the criterion which states that administrative organization should provide for centering responsibility in individuals rather than in groups. The administration of student loan funds is performed chiefly by a standing committee. The larger the institution, the more likely it is that a committee will handle this function. This may indicate that group judgment is considered highly desirable in making loans to students. Student entertainment, such as picnics, dances, excursions, and concerts, are as a rule handled by committees. It seems that these functions would be better administered if responsibility were centered in individuals rather than in groups.

REPRESENTATIVE FUNCTIONS NOT PERFORMED IN SOME TEACHERS COLLEGES

Table XXXV, page 151, shows that some representative functions are not performed in several teachers colleges. Ad-

TABLE XXXIV

STUDENT WELFARE

THE PERFORMANCE OF ADMINISTRATIVE FUNCTIONS IN 22 SMALL, 68 MEDIUM SIZED, 27 LARGE, AND 33 EXTRA LARGE TEACHERS COLLEGES. 1932

Functions and Chief Administrative Officers and Groups Who Usually Perform Them	Percentage of Colleges in Which One Officer or Group Usually Performs the Administrative Function					Percentage of Colleges in Which Two or More Officers or Groups Usually Cooperate in Performing the Function				
	Enrollment					Enrollment				
	Under 300	300 to 799	800 to 1199	1200 or More	All Colleges Combined	Under 300	300 to 799	800 to 1199	1200 or More	All Colleges Combined
1. Formulating policies concerning student welfare										
A. Dean of the college	0	0	0	0	0	4.5	10.3	7.4	15	10
B. Dean of men	0	1.5	0	0	.7	27.2	41.2	48.1	36	39.4
C. Dean of women	4.5	4.4	3.7	9	5.4	50.0	52.9	55.5	33	48.7
D. Director of health	0	0	0	0	0	0	4.4	14.8	9	6.7
E. President	4.5	1.5	0	3	2.0	41.0	32.3	14.8	21	28.1
F. Standing committee	4.5	5.9	22.2	15	10.7	13.6	20.6	3.7	24	17.4
G. Student council	0	1.5	0	0	.7	22.7	10.3	0	15	11.4
2. Approving policies concerning student welfare										
A. Dean of men	0	0	0	0	0	9.1	14.7	14.8	18	14.8
B. Dean of women	4.5	0	0	0	.7	18.2	23.5	22.2	18	22.0
C. Director of health service	0	0	3.7	0	.7	0	1.5	3.7	0	1.4
D. President	45.4	45.6	44.4	42	44.8	36.3	30.9	25.9	24	29.4
E. Special committee	0	0	11.1	6	3.4	4.5	7.5	3.7	9	6.7
3. Providing a list of suitable rooms for students										
A. Dean of men	4.5	0	0	0	.7	22.7	36.8	40.7	42	36.7
B. Dean of women	27.2	13.2	18.5	15	16.7	31.8	42.6	55.5	36	42.0
C. President	4.5	7.5	3.7	6	6.1	9.1	10.3	0	0	6.1
D. Standing committee	0	1.5	11.1	9	4.8	0	4.4	0	6	3.4
4. Supervising student health service										
A. Dean of men	0	0	0	0	0	18.2	17.6	5.7	18	15.4
B. Dean of women	9.1	2.9	0	3	2.8	22.7	27.9	11.1	21	22.8
C. Director of health service	27.2	47.0	66.6	54	49.4	22.7	19.1	14.8	9	16.7
D. Head of department	4.5	1.5	7.4	6	4.1	4.5	0	0	0	.7
5. Helping students find part-time employment										
A. Dean of men	4.5	0	0	0	.7	18.2	32.3	37.0	45	34.1

TABLE XXXIV—*(Continued)*

Functions and Chief Administrative Officers and Groups Who Usually Perform Them	Percentage of Colleges in Which One Officer or Group Usually Performs the Administrative Function					Percentage of Colleges in Which Two or More Officers or Groups Usually Cooperate in Performing the Function				
	Enrollment					Enrollment				
	Under 300	300 to 799	800 to 1199	1200 or More	All Colleges Combined	Under 300	300 to 799	800 to 1199	1200 or More	All Colleges Combined
5. *(Cont'd.)*										
B. Dean of women..	9.1	4.4	0	6	4.8	36.3	38.2	37.0	48	40.0
C. President.......	9.1	2.9	0	0	2.8	31.8	17.6	11.1	9	16.7
D. Standing committee...............	22.7	14.7	44.4	15	21.4	9.1	2.9	3.7	6	4.8
6. Administering policies concernng student loans										
A. Business agent...	9.1	2.9	0	0	2.8	4.5	8.8	25.9	3	10.0
B. Dean of men....	0	0	0	0	0	0	1.5	3.7	18	5.4
C. Dean of women..	4.5	1.5	3.7	0	2.0	9.1	5.9	7.4	21	10.0
D. President.......	13.6	13.2	14.8	3	11.4	18.2	22.1	29.6	15	21.4
E. Standing committee...............	18.2	36.8	37.0	45	36.1	9.1	2.9	3.7	9	5.4
7. Directing student entertainment such as picnics, concerts, dances, excursions, etc.										
A. Dean of men....	0	0	0	0	0	22.7	26.5	18.5	33	26.1
B. Dean of women..	9.1	5.9	11.1	3	6.7	45.4	35.3	36.3	39	37.4
C. Director of student social affairs...	4.5	1.5	7.4	9	4.8	0	7.4	3.7	3	4.8
D. Special committee	37.2	10.3	11.1	12	13.4	4.5	7.4	3.7	3	5.4
E. Standing committee...............	9.1	17.6	18.5	12	15.4	13.6	14.7	25.9	12	16.1
8. Establishing standards for rooms										
A. Dean of men....	4.5	0	0	0	.7	22.7	29.4	44.4	33	32.0
B. Dean of women..	18.2	16.7	14.8	9	14.8	31.8	36.8	55.5	39	40.0
C. President.......	13.6	2.9	0	0	3.4	18.2	13.2	7.4	18	14.1
D. Standing committee...............	4.5	1.5	14.8	9	6.1	4.5	5.9	7.4	9	8.1

This table should be read as follows: Full responsibility for formulating policies concerning student welfare is delegated to the dean of the college by none of the colleges. In cooperation with othe officers this responsibility is delegated to the dean of the college by 4.5% of the colleges enrolling fewer than 300 students, by 10.3% of the colleges enrolling 300 to 799 students, etc.
Consult page 89 for a statement concerning the data in this table.

ministrative organization is justified to the extent that it provides for rendering those services which further the professional education of the students who are preparing themselves for teaching. If an administrative function is not performed in some institutions but performed in others, then it seems reasonable to assume that the internal organizations which neglect the performance of the functions are denying service to their students and staff members or that the institutions which do perform the functions under consideration are rendering services which are not needed. The purpose of this section is to show that some of the functions not performed are such that valuable services are being neglected.

The improvement of the instruction of the staff is quite generally conceded as highly desirable. The probationary members of the staff are usually recent appointees and not entirely familiar with the curricula, the policies of the institution, or best techniques in teaching on the college level. Yet, more than one-third of the colleges investigated report that the probationary staff is not supervised. This means that no attempt is made to help the new member of the staff plan his courses to meet the needs of the institution or to avoid duplication of other courses. It also means that no effort is made to help the new instructor develop courses which are neither too easy nor too difficult. Supervision of instruction should help the new member of the staff develop courses for specific purposes and increase the value of his services to the institution.

In-service training for staff members is not planned in 35 per cent of the colleges which reported. Those administrative organizations which neglect the performance of this function are missing an opportunity to help the various staff members grow and develop in their ability to achieve a higher efficiency in their instructional or administrative duty. It seems reasonable to assume that those institutions which plan a program for the in-service training of their staff members will be more likely to get the specific study on the part of the staff which will result in the attainment of the abilities most valuable to the institution.

Exchange professorships among teachers colleges should provide a means of carrying the best practices from one institution to another. A year's work in an institution, during which an alert faculty member studies and observes the new institution, should provide many ideas for the improvement of his work when he returns to his regular position. Differences in curricula, in administrative organization, and in technique of instruction when observed in one college and discussed and

TABLE XXXV

REPRESENTATIVE ADMINISTRATIVE FUNCTIONS NOT PERFORMED IN SOME
TEACHERS COLLEGES. 1932

Functions Not Performed	Percentages of Colleges Not Performing Some Representative Functions				
	22 Colleges Enrollment Under 300	68 Colleges Enrollment 300–799	27 Colleges Enrollment 800–1199	33 Colleges Enrollment 1200 or Above	All Colleges Combined Enrollment
Supervising the instruction of the probationary members of the staff.........	41.0	35.3	55.5	24.0	38.4
Planning in-service training for staff members.......	41.0	35.3	40.7	24.0	34.8
Arranging exchange professorships................	100.0	79.4	62.9	66.0	77.4
Formulating policies concerning educational research..................	72.6	42.6	48.1	24.0	44.1
Formulating policies concerning extension instruction....................	50.0	44.1	22.2	18.0	35.4
Determining what courses may be offered by correspondence..............	77.2	66.2	44.4	45.0	59.4
Planning adequate housing facilities for staff members	90.8	73.5	66.6	78.0	76.1
Planning staff insurance and retirement funds........	59.0	52.9	81.4	48.0	58.1
Guidance of students in selection of courses to meet placement demands.....	36.3	25.0	14.8	18.0	23.4
Conducting educational conferences for graduates who are teaching in the field..	54.5	54.4	59.2	39.0	52.0
Directing conferences with boards of education.....	59.0	58.8	48.1	39.0	52.8
Providing summaries of cost records for various departmental services.........	31.8	13.2	14.8	12.0	16.1
Requiring independent auditing of financial records	36.3	17.6	22.2	18.0	21.4
Insuring buildings.........	27.2	26.5	33.3	30.0	28.7
Planning adequate housing for maintenance staff....	63.6	58.8	81.4	66.0	65.4
Directing in-service training of maintenance staff.....	36.3	25.0	51.8	24.0	31.4

This table should be read as follows: Supervising the instruction of the probationary members of the staff is not performed in 41% of the colleges enrolling under 300 students, in 35.3% of the colleges enrolling between 300 and 799 stud ents, etc.

evaluated by the staff of another, should result in the elimination of the less desirable and the adoption of the more desirable features. Exchange professorships should make such observation, discussion, and evaluation possible. Yet, according to Table XXXV, only a small percentage of teachers colleges arrange for exchanging professors.

The performance of educational research projects in teachers colleges is omitted in nearly half of the institutions included in this study.   Table XXXV shows that 44 per cent of the colleges have no policies formulated concerning educational research. Such policies are more frequently lacking in the smaller institutions; but, even in the colleges enrolling 1200 or more students, research policies are not formulated in 24 per cent of them.   It seems that practically every teachers college would have some institutional problems which would necessitate research.   The lack of research by an institution indicates that its administration is being carried forward without many of the important facts concerning its specific problems.   Such administration is likely to be less effective than one basing its procedures upon facts which are available through research.

Extension classes and correspondence instruction are not offered in a large percentage of institutions. Since several teachers colleges and universities of high standing offer correspondence instruction which is available to all teachers at a nominal cost, there are probably no urgent reasons why additional institutions should offer courses by mail. Table XXXV shows that approximately 60 per cent of the teachers colleges reporting data for this study do not offer such instruction. Table XXXV shows also that 35 per cent of the teachers colleges offer no instruction through extension classes. Such omission may deny some teachers within the service area of the institution concerned an opportunity to grow and improve themselves professionally.

Faculty morale will be influenced to a large degree by living conditions and by a feeling of security for old age. The planning of adequate housing facilities for staff members should build morale and increase efficiency. Unless suitable houses and apartments are available and high grade homes open to the members of the staff, especially those who are not married, much energy will be wasted by the staff in their efforts to solve the problems of housing. Table XXXV shows that 76 per cent of the institutions plan no faculty housing facilities. Staff insurance and retirement funds should provide a feeling of security and thereby give freedom to the faculty to devote their energy to their tasks of providing professional education for prospective teachers. An institution which neglects to provide a retirement fund for its staff members may thereby encourage their retention in active service long after they have reached an age when their replacement by younger men and women would increase institutional efficiency. A teachers college without insurance and retirement funds for its own staff will probably be less influential in leading the public schools of its service area to adopt a policy of planning retirement funds for their teachers. Table XXXV shows that 58 per cent of the institutions investigated have no insurance and retirement funds for their staff members.

Certain functions performed by some institutions to maintain cordial public relations are entirely neglected in others. Public school officials have a right to expect teachers colleges to train graduates who will meet their needs. Yet, as revealed in Table XXXV, one-fourth of the colleges report that no effort is made to guide students in the selection of courses to meet placement demands. The lack of such guidance is an assumption that college freshmen are able to choose their courses better without faculty guidance. It seems reasonable to assume that the demand for teachers is greater in some fields than in others. Information concerning demand and supply should be available in each institution. If the students are aware of demands made by employers and are guided in the selection of courses to meet those demands, the placement of graduates will be less difficult, and the beginning teacher will be more likely to have specific training in the subject matter he is assigned to teach and better public relations will be established.

Conferences between boards of education and staff members of teachers colleges are a means of promoting cooperation between teachers and board members in putting modern educational theories into practice. Table XXXV shows that such conferences are neglected in more than half of the teachers colleges included in this study. Boards of education, especially in the rural areas, play a dominant part in carrying forward educational procedures. To neglect keeping boards informed concerning the newer movements in education and sympathetic toward them is likely to handicap the teachers and make for less effective schools.

Table XXXV shows that educational conferences for graduates who are teaching in the field are reported by approximately half of the colleges investigated. Leman[1] shows that those colleges which conduct such conferences are enthusiastic concerning the results attained. Such conferences are a means by which beginning teachers may continue their professional growth and improve their techniques and skills. At the same time, conferences such as are here proposed should serve to check the value of the curricula used in the institution.

Some business functions are neglected. Table XXXV shows that one-fourth of the teachers colleges carry no fire insurance for their buildings. It is not within the province of this study to investigate the merits of such a policy. However, it seems reasonable to assume that money to replace losses sustained because of fires may be more easily collected from fire insurance companies than from legislative appropriations.

Summaries of cost records for departmental services makes comparison possible and at the same time locates any excessive expenditures. Table XXXV shows that 16 per cent of the colleges investigated have no such summaries. Without such information, it would seem almost impossible to decide in case of necessary retrenchment which services should be discontinued. If each phase of the institutional program is to be justified on the basis of cost, such summaries are imperative.

Table XXXV shows that one-fifth of the colleges have no independent auditing of financial records. Banks, insurance companies, and business firms require such an audit to protect stockholders and to discover undesirable practices which may be brought to light by accountants from outside the organization. It seems that finances of state institutions merit as careful auditing as those in a private business.

The maintenance staff receives little attention from the administration in several institutions. The services of janitors, engineers, and campus attendants are essential for effective

---

[1]Leman, Grant W., *Professional Adjustment Service for Teachers*, Chap. III, p. 48. Unpublished Doctor's dissertation, New York University, 1932.

college maintenance. Table XXXV shows that one-third of the colleges have no program for in-service training of such employees. Minneapolis,[2] Denver, and other cities have found such courses highly desirable. It seems reasonable to assume that similar results could be obtained by planning a program to improve the efficiency of the maintenance staff.

SUMMARY

1. A study of the performance of 175 different administrative functions in 150 teachers colleges shows that presidents usually retain responsibility for performing more administrative functions than they delegate.

2. State boards of control delegate practically all administrative functions to the presidents.

3. Approval of policies for all groups of administrative functions is usually retained by the president.

4. That group of administrative functions which deals with admission, registration, classification, and records of students is performed to a large extent by the dean, the registrar, and the president.

5. Buildings and grounds management is retained by a large percentage of presidents. The superintendent of buildings and grounds is the president's chief assistant in this group of functions.

6. Business management is kept almost entirely in the hands of the president. Business agents perform the routine management.

7. Presidents retain a large share in controlling and directing classroom instruction.

8. The head of the department is the president's chief assistant in supervising probationary members of the staff.

9. Directors of training are responsible for integration of theory and practice.

10. Institutions offering extension or correspondence courses usually have a special officer to perform the administrative work.

[2]The writer directed a short course for public school janitors and engineers held annually at Greeley, Colorado, during the period from 1925 to 1930 inclusive. Officials from Minneapolis and Denver who had conducted similar courses in their respective systems served as instructors for the course conducted at Greeley. They spoke in high terms of the splendid results attained in similar courses in their respective cities.

11. Presidents report that they are their own chief research workers.

12. Those administrative functions which concern the personnel relations of members of the faculty are in nearly all cases under the immediate direction and control of the presidents.

13. There is a predominant practice of delegating placement and adjustment service to one individual, the director of placement.

14. Presidents usually hold themselves responsible for doing or directing those activities which mean contacts with individuals and organizations outside the college.

15. Registrars and standing committees are more frequently responsible for publications and publicity than other officials.

16. Functions pertaining to student organizations are largely delegated to committees and department heads.

17. Teachers colleges of all sizes usually make a greater use of committees than of administrative officers in the direction and control of student social activities.

18. Presidents usually delegate functions regarding student standards of conduct except the approval of policies.

19. The dean of men, the dean of women, and the student council share in the administration of student standards of conduct.

20. Directors of training are dominantly in control of student teaching.

21. Department heads have only a small share of responsibility in student teaching.

22. Many presidents delegate functions so that two or more officers share in the performance of the duties involved.

23. With the exception of the approval of policies, those administrative functions which pertain to student welfare are performed by other officials than the president in nearly all teachers colleges.

24. Representative functions frequently not performed in teachers colleges include the following:
    A. Supervising the instruction of the probationary members of the staff.
    B. Planning in-service training for staff members.
    C. Arranging exchange professorships.
    D. Formulating policies concerning educational research.

E. Formulating policies concerning extension instruction.
F. Determining what courses may be offered by correspondence.
G. Planning adequate housing facilities for staff members.
H. Planning staff insurance and retirement funds.
I. Guiding students in selection of courses to meet placement demands.
J. Conducting educational conferences for graduates who are teaching in the field.
K. Directing conferences with boards of education.
L. Providing summaries of cost records for various departmental services.
M. Requiring independent auditing of financial records.
N. Insuring buildings.
O. Planning adequate housing for maintenance staff.
P. Directing in-service training of maintenance staff.

CRITICAL EVALUATION

The fact that many of the presidents of the institutions included in this study usually perform more administrative functions than they delegate may indicate a reluctance on their part to delegate responsibility to their subordinate officers. On the other hand, the fact that some presidents do delegate responsibility for performance of functions is evidence that the principle of delegating functions is successfully practiced in some teachers colleges. There is little justification for presidents holding themselves responsible for many of the functions reported by some institutions as chiefly presidential responsibility. Assigning classrooms to instructors, planning programs for assemblies, evaluating high school credits, managing the buildings and grounds staff, and disposing of salvaged materials are functions which some presidents perform. These functions do not seem to be so complex that the chief executive should give personal attention to their control and management. Retention by the presidents of such functions is bound to give them duties during the performance of which they will be prevented from giving attention to the development of institutional and administrative policies. Freedom from such duties is rated as highly desirable by 90 per cent of the jury of teachers college presidents which evaluated the criteria for this study.   Learned and Bagley,[3] in writing on this subject, emphasize in these words the necessity of freeing the president from a multiplicity of duties: "As educational institutions have become larger and more complex, the mass of intersecting relations has made it imperative that the guiding mind be set free for close, detached study of principles that govern all of this and other professional procedures; that time be provided for abundant outside observation, comparison, and reflection; and that he be so lifted above detail as to serve steadily, without waste or hurry, his main function—to be the inspiring power and illuminating interpreter behind the whole organization."

Many presidents do not use faculty judgments concerning matters of instruction.   Presidents formulate as well as approve instructional policies.   The omission of the staff in the formulating of policies is neglecting the use of special talents and group experience which the faculty might possess.   It was previously pointed out in Chapter II that the jury evaluating the administrative criteria gives a high index rating to that criterion which states that the faculty should participate in formulating policies concerning instruction.   The faculty members from their continuous working with instruction should have a contribution to make in the formulation of instructional policies.   To fail to provide in the internal organization a means for utilizing this contribution not only reduces the efficiency of the institution, but probably lowers the morale of those who carry out instructional policies.

The training school is frequently mentioned in the catalogs of the teachers colleges included in this study as the "heart of the institution."   All professional training which precedes the period of practice is meant to strengthen the student for that critical period of teaching.   Yet the training staff is not reported from a single institution as having any share in the formulation of policies regarding campus instruction.   On the other hand, the faculty as a whole help in but few institutions in formulating instructional policies in the training school. Those administrative organizations which neglect the use of the training school staff in formulating policies for campus

---

[3]Learned, W. S. and Bagley, W. C., *The Professional Preparation of Teachers for the American Public Schools*, p. 273.

instruction and likewise neglect the use of the faculty as a whole in formulating policies regarding instruction in the training school are violating the criterion which states that the faculty should participate in formulating instructional policies.

Only a few institutions report that policies are referred to the state board of control for approval. Such omission is in opposition to the criterion which states that administrative organization should provide for the approval of policies by the state board of control. As was pointed out in Chapter II, the president needs to protect himself and the institution by securing approval of policies. The organization and stating of policies in preparation for submitting them for approval is bound to promote careful consideration and a more definite formulation of the policy. The presidents report that they approve policies. This gives them an opportunity to make the final decisions regarding what policies will be submitted to state boards for approval. This is in accord with the validated criteria.

There are administrative councils in 70 per cent of the institutions included in this study. Yet they have practically no share in formulating policies or in performance of functions. The validated criterion on this point gives a high index rating to such a council as an advisory group. It seems reasonable to assume that such a council could render its best service in cooperating in the formulation of policies. The tables in Chapter V show that such cooperation exists in but few colleges. It seems safe to conclude that administrative councils are not used in many of the institutions where they exist.

An analysis of all the tables in Chapter V emphasizes that two or more officers share responsibilities for performance of functions in many institutions. The sharing of such responsibility is in opposition to the criterion which states that responsibility should be centered in individuals rather than in groups. As was pointed out in Chapter II, failure to center responsibility in individuals prevents giving credits for tasks well performed or censure for duty neglected. Such sharing of responsibility in the performance of functions can be justified only when the duties are too heavy for one officer or so complicated that group judgment is desirable.

CHAPTER VI

SUMMARY AND RECOMMENDATIONS

CHAPTER I introduces the study, states the general problem, and describes the procedures used in the investigation. Chapter II states and discusses criteria for internal administrative organization. An evaluation of the criteria by a jury of teachers college presidents who were named by their colleagues as superior administrators is shown in tabular form in this chapter. Chapter III contains a discussion of the present status of committees in teachers colleges, conflicting viewpoints concerning use of committees in administration, and the procedures used by presidents of teachers colleges in administering committees. Chapter IV shows the interrelations between administrative officers, with special reference to the average amount of classroom instruction assigned to members of the administrative staff, the combination of offices held, and the administrative responsibility of officers. Chapter V points out which officers usually perform the various administrative functions in colleges of different sizes. This chapter shows the percentage of institutions in which one officer usually performs the different functions and the percentage of institutions in which two or more officers share in performing functions. This chapter also shows which functions are usually performed by groups rather than individuals. On the whole it gives a picture of the way presidents use their assistants in administering the functions of teachers colleges.

I. VALIDATING CRITERIA FOR ADMINISTRATIVE ORGANIZATION

Twenty criteria for the internal administrative organization of teachers colleges were derived from the literature in the field and from administrative practices in teachers colleges. A jury of thirty teachers college presidents rated these criteria as follows:

1. Highly desirable.
2. Desirable.
3. Of no particular value but not undesirable.
4. Undesirable.
5. Harmful.

The jury was in agreement concerning most of the criteria. The composite rating indicated that the jury of teachers college presidents believes that internal administrative organization should provide for the following:

1. Performance of essentially the same administrative functions in all teachers colleges.
2. Greater specialization in administration as the enrollment becomes greater.
3. Freedom for the instructional staff to teach in their various departments without being overburdened with administrative duties.
4. Freedom from the performance of a multiplicity of duties by the president.
5. Utilization of an administrative council in an advisory capacity.
6. Faculty representation on the administrative council.
7. Special committees for investigations requiring special study.
8. Selection of special and standing committees by president.
9. Constant membership and chairmanship in standing committees.
10. A fixed procedure for replacing membership in standing committees.
11. Participation by the whole faculty in suggesting or formulating policies concerning instruction.
12. Grouping of related functions under control of administrative officers who in turn are responsible to president.
13. The centering of responsibility in individuals rather than in groups.
14. Approval of policies by the state board of control.
15. The making of final decisions by the president after policies have been approved by the state board.

To a large extent there is agreement among the jury of presidents that some criteria would lead to undesirable or harmful administrative conditions.   These criteria are those which provide for:

1. Selection of special and standing committees by the faculty.
2. Providing standing committees for all administrative functions.

There are some criteria which the majority of the jury rates as of no particular value but not undesirable.   These are:

1. Using department heads for an administrative council.
2. Providing for faculty approval of all major administrative policies.

One criterion in particular shows a sharp difference of opinion. Some members of the jury believe that administrative organization should provide few or no standing committees for the organization of administrative functions.   Nearly as large a group of the jurors believe that administrative organization should provide standing committees for the administration of all major groups of functions.

II. COMMITTEES IN ADMINISTRATIVE ORGANIZATION

A survey of the present status of committees in teachers colleges shows an average of approximately ten standing committees for each institution investigated.   The larger colleges usually have a greater number of committees than the smaller ones.   Some committees are more prevalent in teachers colleges than others.   Those found most frequently deal with:

1. Entertainment and lyceum.
2. Student activities.
3. Student social affairs.
4. Construction and reconstruction of the curriculum.

There are six committees whose frequency of occurrence in general increases as the enrollment increases.   These committees deal with the functions involved in:

1. College publications.
2. Curriculum.
3. Extension and correspondence.

4. Library service.
5. Placement of graduates.
6. Student publications.

There are no committees which decrease in frequency of occurrence as enrollment increases.

Administrative councils are organized in 70 per cent of the colleges included in the study. Nearly all councils are chosen by the president to serve in an advisory capacity. A few institutions have administrative councils which consist of department heads. A few others organize the council to include faculty representatives.

The literature dealing with organization in teachers colleges presents two conflicting viewpoints concerning the use of committees in administration. One viewpoint contends that the chief function of committees is to study problems and recommend policies. Such committees would be appointed when needed and discharged when their investigation was completed. The second viewpoint holds that committees should be appointed to administer functions. Such committees would have both legislative and administrative powers and serve continuously.

Procedures used by presidents in the administration of committees are as follows:

1. Presidents usually appoint committees.
2. In a few institutions the faculty selects committees.
3. A large percentage of presidents retain ex-officio membership in all standing committees.
4. Nearly all committees make investigations.
5. Practically all committees made recommendations.
6. Nearly half of the committees initiate policies through legislation.
7. Approximately 75 per cent of all committees administer policies.
8. The decisions made by 80 per cent of the committees are subject to reversal by the president.
9. There is a regular way for changing the membership in nearly all committees.
10. There is a tendency to retain the same individuals on committees.

11. Approximately one committee in four is given a written list of duties.
12. A few more than half of the committees report in writing.
13. There are some administrative officers on approximately 75 per cent of the committees.
14. Presidents report that nearly all committees function annually.

III. INTERRELATIONS OF ADMINISTRATIVE OFFICERS

Twenty-six different administrative officers are found in 5 per cent or more of the colleges which furnished data for this study. Those officers, other than the president, found most frequently are: business agent, dean of men, dean of women, director of athletics, director of health, director of placement, director of training, librarian, registrar, and superintendent of buildings and grounds.   Officers established in only a few institutions are: director of adjustment, director of housing, director of instruction, director of personnel, director of research, director of student activities, director of social affairs, and vice-president. There is a positive correlation between the size of the institution and the number of administrative officers.   All the colleges combined average approximately twelve administrative officers each.

The administrative officers average fairly heavy teaching loads.   On the whole, the teaching load of administrative officers is heavier in the smaller institutions.   But, even in the extra large institutions, there are several officers who average teaching approximately half of a regular load.   For all colleges combined the following officers average teaching ten hours or more per week: dean of men, director of athletics, director of research, and editor of publications.

In general, two offices are not combined under the direction of one official.   However, there are several combinations which occur quite frequently.   These are:

1. College dean and registrar.
2. Dean of men and director of athletics.
3. Dean of women and director of student social activities.
4. Dean of women and director of housing.
5. Director of extension and director of placement.
6. Director of placement and director of training.

7. Director of training and director of adjustment.
8. Registrar and business agent.
9. Business agent and superintendent of buildings and grounds.

Practically all officers are administratively responsible to the president. However, in a few institutions officers whose duties are closely related are grouped under the administrative direction of an official who in turn is responsible to the president. In such colleges the chief storekeeper, chief accountant, and superintendent of buildings and grounds are usually responsible to the business agent. In some colleges the dean of women is administratively responsible for directing the officer in charge of housing, the college nurse and the director of social activities. The director of training frequently has a group of officers who are responsible to him. These officers are the principals of the training schools, the director of adjustment, and the director of placement. On the whole, administrative responsibility to anyone other than the president is not the regular relationship.

IV. THE PERFORMANCE OF ADMINISTRATIVE FUNCTIONS

Presidents usually retain more administrative functions for performance than they delegate. Although the state board of control gives the majority of presidents a free hand, they in turn often delegate only partial responsibility, thus holding themselves responsible for the performance of a multiplicity of duties. The approval of administrative policies is retained by nearly all presidents. Such retention keeps control where responsibility is placed.

Business management is kept almost entirely in the hands of the president in a majority of institutions. Business agents perform routine functions. Budgeting, financial accounting, property accounting, payroll management, and purchasing are functions which many presidents give personal attention. Buildings and grounds management is retained by a large percentage of presidents who make use of a superintendent of buildngs and grounds as a chief assistant. Landscaping, salvaging material, sanitation, storage and distribution of supplies, and the in-service training of the buildings and grounds staff are usually delegated to the superintendent of buildings and grounds, although some presidents hold themselves responsible for these functions.

Functions pertaining to instruction are generally not directed by a single head except in so far as the president does the directing himself. Nearly all supervision of instruction is done by the president, the college dean, and the head of the department. Such supervision is omitted entirely in many institutions. The librarian and president often plan improvement of library service without assistance from department heads or the faculty as a whole. Directors of training are usually responsible for integration of theory and practice. Extension instruction is omitted in many institutions. When offered, such instruction is usually directed by an officer who does not have control of similar instruction on the campus. Student teaching as a function is quite completely delegated to the director of training and his staff with little or no provision for the faculty as a whole to share in formulating policies for such teaching.

Personnel functions are not as a general thing grouped for administrative control. The presidents perform many personnel functions. Registrars, deans of men, deans of women, directors of placement, directors of health service, and committees are all used, but little evidence is reported to show that such officers and committees are working to develop unified programs. The fact that the various officers in an institution who handle different phases of personnel are directly responsible to the president is indicative that separate rather than unified personnel programs are being developed in teachers colleges.

Only a few presidents delegate to subordinate officials functions pertaining to public relations. Many of the teachers colleges investigated do not have a program planned to build good will on the part of the public. However, in those institutions having such a program the presidents direct it themselves. Presidents, more than other officials, visit public schools and arrange for staff lectures and technical service by staff members. The president is the dominant force in organizing alumni associations. Conferences for boards of education and for teachers, if arranged at all, usually are arranged by the president. In short, off-campus contacts are generally handled by the presidents.

Staff administration concerning faculty personnel relations

is handled almost entirely by the presidents with some assistance from heads of departments and college deans.   Presidents quite generally locate candidates for positions, offer them contacts, and determine their academic ranking.   If there is a program of in-service training for staff members, it is planned by the president.   Many important functions concerning faculty personnel relations are not provided for in administrative organizations.   Insurance and retirement funds for staff members, the planning of housing facilities, and the arranging for exchange professorships are frequently neglected, but, when included as a part of administrative functions, the president usually performs the duties connected therewith.

V. THE CONFORMITY OF PRACTICE WITH CRITERIA

Validated criteria stated in Chapter II and institutional practices analyzed in Chapters III, IV, and V make possible a summary and evaluation by institutions of present organizations in the light of approved criteria.   Table XXXVI, page 169, shows such a summary.   This table is based upon data furnished by teachers college presidents.   In tabulating data to show whether or not the requirements of the validated criteria were met, arbitrary standards were used.   These standards are stated in the following summary:

1. *Are important administrative functions omitted?*

Whenever institutions reported that they omitted six or more functions, such as providing supervision for probationary members of the staff, neglecting to plan in-service training for staff members, providing no summaries of cost records for departmental services, and other similar functions, that college was listed as not meeting the criterion that administrative organization should provide for the performance of essentially the same administrative functions.   Approximately 73 per cent of the institutions omit six or more such functions.

2. *Are officers given an opportunity to specialize in administration?*

Whenever three or more officers within an institution were listed as teaching more than eight hours each, that institution was tabulated as not providing an opportunity for its officers to specialize in administration.   Approximately half of the teachers colleges investigated have three or more officers whose teaching load exceeds eight hours per week in addition to their administrative load.

3. *Is the instructional staff overburdened with administrative duties?*

Colleges tabulated as overburdening their instructional staff with administrative duties are those in which the administrative officers teach on an average of eight hours or more per week and whose staff members serve on committees which administer policies.   Approximately 16 per cent of the colleges included in this study overburden their instructional staff in accordance with this standard.

4. *Does the president perform a multiplicity of duties?*

Those institutions whose presidents reported that they performed or shared in the performance of more than half of the administrative functions as stated in Chapter V were tabulated as institutions whose administrative organization does not provide freedom for the president to consider the larger problems of the college.   There are according to this standard 36 per cent of the teachers college presidents who perform a multiplicity of duties which may occupy their time to such an extent that major attention cannot be given to the development of administrative and institutional policies.

5. *Is an administrative council organized?*

Seventy per cent of the colleges reporting data for this study state that they have an organized administrative council.   Of the 106 councils reported there are seventy-one whose members are appointed by the president.   The faculty chooses representatives for only five of the organized councils.   Fourteen councils are made up of department heads.   In the light of approved criteria there are forty-four colleges which should give attention to the desirability of an organized administrative council. Since faculty representation on the administrative council is given a high rating, 101 of the institutions having councils should give careful consideration to the desirability of faculty representation.

CHARACTERISTICS OF INTERNAL ADMINISTRATIVE ORGANIZATION IN 150 TEACHERS COLLEGES. 1932

Questions Indicating Characteristics of Internal Organization	22 Colleges Enrollment Under 300			68 Colleges Enrollment 300–799			27 Colleges Enrollment 800–1199			33 Colleges Enrollment 1200 or More			All Colleges Combined		
	Yes	No	% Yes	Yes	No	% Yes	Yes	No	% Yes	Yes	No	% Yes	Yes	No	% Yes
Are important administrative functions omitted?	18	4	81.7	52	16	76.4	21	6	77.7	18	15	54.0	109	41	72.8
Are officers given an opportunity to specialize in administration?	12	10	54.5	32	36	47.0	15	12	55.5	17	16	51.0	76	74	50.7
Is the instructional staff overburdened with administrative duties?	3	19	13.6	13	55	19.1	4	23	14.8	4	29	12.0	24	126	16.1
Does the president perform a multiplicity of duties?	17	6	77.2	30	38	44.1	5	22	18.5	2	31	6.0	54	96	36.1
Is an administrative council organized?	8	14	35.3	50	18	73.5	18	9	66.6	30	3	90.0	106	44	70.7
Does the president select the members of the administrative council?	7	1	87.5 *	39	11	78.0 *	12	6	66.6 *	13	17	43.3 *	71	35	67.0 *
Is the faculty represented on the council?	0	8	0	4	46	8.0 *	0	18	0 *	1	29	3.3 *	5	101	5.0 *
Are heads of departments ex-officio members of the administrative council?	0	8	0	6	44	12.0	2	16	11.0	6	24	20.0	14	92	13.2
Are special committees appointed to investigate topics requiring special study?	16	6	72.6	61	7	89.7	26	1	96.2	30	3	90.0	133	17	88.7
Does the president select standing and special committees?	16	6	72.6	66	2	97.0	26	1	96.2	30	3	90.0	138	12	92.0
Does the faculty or representative of the faculty select standing and special committees?	0	22	0	3	65	4.4	1	26	3.7	2	31	6.0	6	144	4.0
Do standing committees administer policies?	14	8	63.6	55	13	80.9	25	2	92.5	28	5	84.0	122	28	81.4
Is there a regular procedure for changing committee membership?	12	10	54.5	52	16	76.4	21	6	77.7	30	3	90.0	116	34	77.3
Does the whole faculty participate in formulating policies concerning instruction?	11	11	50.0	13	55	19.1	3	24	11.1	11	22	33.3	38	112	25.4
Does the faculty approve all major administrative policies?	3	19	13.6	1	67	1.5	0	27	0	1	32	3.0	5	145	3.4
Are related functions grouped under the direction of an officer who in turn is responsible to the president?	7	15	31.8	25	43	36.8	12	15	44.4	21	12	63.0	65	85	43.4
Are responsibilities centered in individuals rather than in groups?	16	6	72.6	42	26	61.7	19	8	70.3	26	7	78.0	103	47	68.7
Does administrative organization provide for approval of policies by the state board of control?	13	9	59.0	45	23	66.2	17	10	62.9	32	1	96.0	107	43	71.4
Does the president make final decisions after policies have been approved by the state board of control?	18	4	81.7	56	12	82.3	23	4	85.1	27	6	81.0	124	26	82.8

*The percentage below the asterisk is based upon the number of institutions which have administrative councils rather than the total number of colleges investigated.

6. *How does practice regarding the use of committees agree with validated criteria?*

Special committees are appointed to investigate topics requiring special study in 89 per cent of the colleges. The president selects standing and special committees in 92 per cent of the institutions. Both of these procedures are rated highly in the validated criteria. In six institutions the faculty selects special and standing committees. This procedure is rated in the criteria as negative and harmful. In 77 per cent of the teachers colleges standing committees administer policies. The jury of teachers college presidents gave a negative rating for administration by committees. However, Table II, page 11, shows that several jurors rated such administration as highly desirable. Committee membership is changed in 77 per cent of the colleges by regular procedure. Administrative provision for a regular procedure to change committee membership is given a low but positive rating by the jury.

7. *Does the whole faculty participate in formulating policies concerning instruction?*

Thirty-eight teachers colleges investigated are so organized that the entire faculty participates in suggesting or formulating policies concerning instruction. The jury rated such participation as highly desirable; yet there are 112 presidents who report that the faculty as a whole does not participate in the formulation of instructional policies in the institutions over which they preside.

8. *Does the faculty approve all major administrative policies?*

The jury rated the provision for approval of all major administrative policies as of no particular value but probably not undesirable. Only five of the 150 colleges investigated reported that the policies formulated for the administration of the various groups of functions are approved by the faculty.

9. *Are related functions grouped under the direction of an officer who in turn is responsible to the president?*

The practice of grouping related functions under the direction of an officer who in turn is responsible to the president was rated by the jury as a highly desirable administrative condition.

Such grouping was found in 43 per cent of the institutions included in this study. Institutions listed as not grouping such functions are those which reported the chief accountant not administratively responsible to the business agent, and the principals of the training schools not responsible to the director of training.

10. *Are responsibilities centered in individuals rather than in groups?*

Those colleges which reported that a majority of their administrative functions were performed either by committees or by two or more administrative officers who shared jointly in the responsibility for the performance of the function, were tabulated as centering responsibility in groups rather than in individuals. According to this standard there are forty-seven colleges which center responsibility in individuals. Provision for centering responsibility in individuals rather than in groups is rated as highly desirable by the jury of teachers college presidents.

11. *Does administrative organization provide for the approval of policies by the state board of control?*

One hundred and seven institutions which furnished data for this investigation report that the state board of control approved or rejected proposed administrative policies. Forty-three institutions make no mention of the state board of control as an authority which approved their administrative policies. The majority of the members of the jury of teachers college presidents rate the provision for such approval as highly desirable.

12. *Does the president make final decisions after policies have been approved by the state board of control?*

Those institutions in which the president either alone or in cooperation with one subordinate official approves policies of administration were tabulated as institutions in which the president makes final decisions. There are 124 such colleges in this study. Twenty-six institutions report that final decisions are made by the faculty vote, vote of the administrative council, or vote of the executive committee. The jury of teachers college presidents are almost unanimous in rating provision for making final decisions by the president as a highly desirable administrative condition.

VI.　RECOMMENDATIONS

1. Table XXXV, page 151, shows that several administrative functions now performed in some teachers colleges are omitted in others.　It is therefore recommended that presidents analyze the internal administrative organization of their respective staffs and either provide for functions now omitted or satisfy themselves that it is not desirable for the college in question to perform certain functions at this time.　This procedure should prevent the neglect of functions which contribute to administrative efficiency and help to establish reasons why some functions which are ordinarily performed are not desirable in teachers colleges.

2. Table II, page 11, shows a high positive index rating for the participation by the faculty in the formulation of policies which concern instruction.　Table XXXIII, page 143, shows that such participation is very limited.　To improve this situation a committee on instruction is recommended.　Construction and reconstruction of the curricula for college classes and the demonstration schools would be the responsibility of this committee.　Such a committee, under the chairmanship of the director of instruction and made up of representatives of various groups, would provide a means for faculty participation in formulating instructional policies.　All members of the staff should be organized into groups whose instructional problems are closely related.　Through discussion meetings of these groups it would be possible to develop various suggestions which could be carried to the committee on instruction for consideration.　The deliberations of this committee, influenced by previous group meetings in which all members of the staff have participated, should develop a unified and well-balanced instructional policy which would be carried out in the classrooms and in the training school.

3. Table II shows that the jury of teachers college presidents favor an administrative council to advise the president concerning the formulation of policies and the making of administrative

decisions.   They rate selection of the members of the administrative council by the president equally high with faculty representation on the council.   An administrative council serving to advise the president is recommended.   The majority of the council should be chosen by the president, and the remainder should be chosen by the faculty.   The council should advise, present different viewpoints, and often suggest possible alternative policies; but never usurp the right of the president to make the final decisions.

4. Chapter V shows that many presidents perform a multiplicity of routine duties.   It is recommended that presidents delegate all administrative functions which are routine in nature unless the performance of those functions aids in understanding the larger problems of administration.

5. Table VII, page 53, shows that many officers carry a heavy teaching load in addition to their regular administrative duties. Such a combination forces the officers involved to keep up in both instruction and administration.   It is therefore recommended that administrative organization provide for assigning full-time administrative loads to officers unless classroom instruction will contribute directly to the administrative efficiency of the officer concerned.   A director of instruction would probably be more efficient because of his classroom teaching. A director of placement might use classroom instruction as an effective means of getting acquainted with students whom he will recommend for positions at some subsequent date.   Situations of this nature justify combining instruction and administration.

6. Since, according to the validated criteria, responsibility should be centered in individuals rather than groups, committees for administration of functions are not recommended. Special committees to investigate special topics are approved by the jury of teachers college presidents.   Such committees are recommended.   They should be appointed by the president.   The duties and functions of special committees should be formulated and stated in writing.   Special committees should be required to report their findings and recommendations in writing.   When their work is completed they should be officially discharged.

7. A standing committee on student conduct is recommended.

174 Administrative Organization in Teachers Colleges

It is justified as a standing committee because of the inherent nature of its functions. The student conduct committee needs to be organized as a standing committee in order to serve quickly in rendering group judgment in an emergency.

8. An analysis of the tables in Chapter V reveals that a substantial percentage of the institutions included in this study delegate functions in such a way that two or more officers share in the responsibility for their performance. In order to center responsibility in individuals rather than in groups, it is recommended that functions be delegated for performance to one officer. In large institutions each administrative officer should have secretaries and assistants whom he can hold responsible for performing definite duties.

9. Data presented in the tables in Chapter IV show that a very large majority of officers are administratively responsible to the president. In order to relieve the president of a multiplicity of interviews and routine functions and to encourage an integrated administrative program, it is recommended that all administration functions be grouped into five administrative divisions. Figure I gives in detail a proposed grouping. Such a grouping stresses public relations, instruction, personnel, business and finance, and faculty personnel relations. This functional grouping provides an opportunity for the administrative head of an institution to make one type of service paramount within each administrative division and to make possible the appointment of divisional directors when finances permit an administrative staff. All services in which first consideration must be given to others than students or staff are grouped in the public relations division. The instruction division includes those functions which concern what to teach and how to teach. The director of the division of instruction under such a functional grouping would work almost entirely with faculty members. The functions grouped in the personnel division are those which require constant contacts with students in all their college relationships, with the exception of classroom instruction and library service. Those functions which concern property and financial management are grouped in the division of business and finance. In addition to these four divisions there is a fifth division provided in the recommendation which groups all of those activities related to

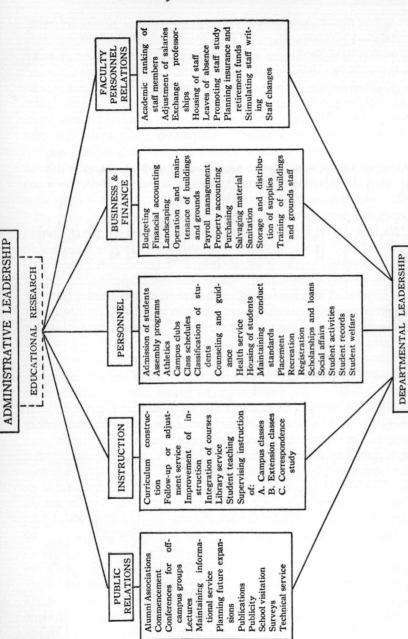

FIGURE I. Functional Grouping Recommended or the Internal Administrative Organization or Teachers Colleges.

the upbuilding and maintenance of faculty morale into a faculty personnel relations division.

It is believed that this grouping provides for all the important administrative functions and at the same time encourages specialization upon the part of the administrative officers who are assisting the president. Such a grouping is readily adaptable to any teachers college. Even in very small institutions where the president may be compelled to perform the administrative functions without a staff of officers to assist him, such a grouping makes possible the assignment of clerks and secretaries to work with functions which are closely related. In institutions permitting the employment of administrative officers it provides for the delegation of a group of related functions to officers who may specialize in a particular field. At the same time such functional delegation provides for fixing responsibility and informing the members of the staff relative to the authority of administrative assistants. In large institutions such grouping provides for administrative leadership of related functions and the appointment of subordinate officers to assist divisional directors. It is recommended that such subordinate officers be administratively responsible to the director of the division in which each works. It is believed that such administrative responsibility will relieve the president of a multiplicity of duties and develop an integrated administration with a minimum of duplication of effort, and at the same time provide for the president to retain direct control of those divisions which will give him an opportunity to make his greatest contribution in accordance with his qualifications.

BIBLIOGRAPHY

AGNEW, W. D. *The Administration of Professional Schools for Teachers.* Warwick and York, Inc., Baltimore, 1924.

BARNARD, HENRY. *Normal Schools and Other Institutions, Agencies, and Means Designed for the Professional Education of Teachers,* Vol. I, 1851. Reprinted by Colorado State Teachers College, Greeley, Colo., 1929.

BRUNSTETTER, M. R. *Business Management in School Systems of Different Sizes.* Bureau of Publications, Teachers College, Columbia University, New York, 1931.

CAPEN, SAMUEL P. AND STEVENS, EDWIN B. *Report of a Survey of the University of Nevada.* Bureau of Education Bulletin (1917), No. 19. Department of the Interior, Washington, D. C., 1917.

CHARTERS, W. W. AND WAPLES, DOUGLAS. *The Commonwealth Teacher Training Study.* The University of Chicago Press, Chicago, Ill., 1929.

COLLIER, CLARENCE B. *The Dean of the State Teachers College.* Bureau of Publications, George Peabody College for Teachers, Nashville, Tenn., 1926.

EVENDEN, E. S. "The Improvement of College Teaching." *Teachers College Record,* Vol. XXIX, pp. 587–596, April, 1928.

FLOWERS, JOHN GARLAND. *The Content of Student-Teaching Courses Designed for the Training of Secondary Teachers in State Teachers Colleges.* Bureau of Publications, Teachers College, Columbia University, New York, 1932.

FOSTER, WILLIAM T. "Faculty Participation in College Government." *School and Society,* Vol. III, No. 69, p. 596, April 22, 1916.

HALL-QUEST, A. L. *Professional Secondary Education in Teachers Colleges.* Bureau of Publications, Teachers College, Columbia University, New York, 1925.

HUGHES, WILLIAM LEONARD. *The Administration of Health and Physical Education for Men in Colleges and Universities.* Bureau of Publications, Teachers College, Columbia University, New York, 1932.

JUDD, CHARLES H. *et al. Report of a Survey of the State Institutions of Higher Learning in Indiana.* Board of Public Printing, State House, Indianapolis, Ind., December, 1926.

KENT, RAYMOND A. *Higher Education in America.* Ginn and Company, Boston, 1930.

KLEIN, ARTHUR J. *Survey of Land Grant Colleges and Universities,* Vol. I. Office of Education Bulletin (1930), No. 9. Department of Interior, Washington, D. C., 1930.

LEARNED, W. S. AND BAGLEY, W. C. *The Professional Preparation of Teachers for American Public Schools.* The Carnegie Foundation for the Advancement of Teaching, New York, 1920.

LEMAN, GRANT W. *Professional Adjustment Service for Teachers.* Unpublished Doctor's Dissertation, New York University, 1932.

177

LEONARD, R. J., EVENDEN, E. S., AND O'REAR, F. B. *Survey of Higher Education for the United Lutheran Church in America.* Bureau of Publications, Teachers College, Columbia University, New York, 1929.

LINDSAY, E. E. AND HOLLAND, E. O. *College and University Administration.* The Macmillan Company, New York, 1930.

MCVEY, F. L. "Administrative Relations in College." *School and Society*, Vol. 15, pp. 705–709, December 8, 1928.

Missouri Survey of Higher Education. State Survey Commission, Jefferson City, Mo., 1929.

MOEHLMAN, ARTHUR B. *A Survey of the Needs of the Michigan State Normal Schools.* Department of Public Instruction, Lansing, Mich., 1922.

O'REAR, F. B. *The Duties of the Registrar.* Inland Printing and Binding Company, Springfield, Mo., 1925.

REEDER, W. G. *The Business Administration of a School System.* Ginn and Company, Boston, 1927.

REEVES, FLOYD W. AND RUSSELL, JOHN DALE. *College Organization and Administration.* Board of Education, Disciples of Christ, Indianapolis, Ind., 1929.

Report of the Committee of Ten on Secondary School Studies. American Book Company, New York, 1894.

RUTLEDGE, SAMUEL A. *The Development of Guiding Principles for the Administration of Teachers Colleges and Normal Schools.* Bureau of Publications, Teachers College, Columbia University, New York, 1930.

SHERROD, C. C. *The Administration of State Teachers Colleges through Faculty Committees.* Bureau of Publications, George Peabody College for Teachers, Nashville, Tenn., 1925.

Survey of Education in Utah. Bureau of Education Bulletin (1926) No. 18. Department of the Interior, Washington, D. C., 1926.

TAYLOR, ROBERT B. *Principles of School Supply Management.* Bureau of Publications, Teachers College, Columbia University, New York, 1926.

THEISEN, W. W. *The City Superintendent and the Board of Education.* Bureau of Publications, Teachers College, Columbia University, New York, 1917.

UNITED STATES BUREAU OF EDUCATION, Bulletin No. 35, 1918. Department of the Interior, Washington, D. C., 1918.

APPENDIX A

NATIONAL SURVEY
OF THE
EDUCATION OF TEACHERS

Criteria For Evaluating Internal Administrative Organization in Teachers Colleges

UNITED STATES DEPARTMENT OF THE INTERIOR,
OFFICE OF EDUCATION, WASHINGTON, D. C.

DIRECTIONS CONCERNING RATING

TWENTY criteria for evaluating internal administrative organization in teachers colleges are stated on the next two pages. They were formulated from the literature pertaining to internal administrative organization and from a study of present practice in teachers colleges. Some of the criteria contradict others in the list. Hence, they cannot all be valid. A group of teachers college presidents designated as superior administrative officers are being requested to rate the criteria and through jury judgment help determine which are valid. It is especially desirable to learn which of these criteria, if any, are dependent upon financial support for validity. Hence, two reactions are requested for each criterion. In making the first reaction, please assume reasonably adequate financial support. In making your second reaction, assume that financial support is curtailed or limited.

Please bear in mind that these criteria are limited to internal administrative organization in teachers colleges. They are not intended as adequate in scope for guidance in the administration of all functions.

Space is provided at the bottom of this page for comments and suggestions. Your cooperation and a prompt response will be appreciated greatly.

Yours sincerely,
ROBERT H. MORRISON,
Tabulator.

COMMENTS AND SUGGESTIONS

Signature...................................
Address...................................

*When completed, please return to the Department of the Interior,
Office of Education, Washington, D. C.*

[Pages 1 and 2 of the Original Form]

179

A STATEMENT OF CRITERIA

	Financial Support Reasonably Adequate					Financial Support Curtailed or Limited				
Please write (X) in the columns to the right opposite the word or words which best describe your judgment of the administrative condition represented by each criterion below. First, assume financial support reasonably adequate. Second, assume financial support curtailed or limited.	Highly Desirable	Desirable	Of No Particular Value But Not Undesirable	Undesirable	Harmful	Highly Desirable	Desirable	Of No Particular Value But Not Undesirable	Undesirable	Harmful
	1	2	3	4	5	1	2	3	4	5
1. Administrative organization should provide for the performance of essentially the same administrative functions in all teachers colleges. An administrative function in this criterion refers to such activities as classification of students, preparing the budget, etc.										
2. As the enrollment becomes greater, administrative organization should provide for greater specialization of duties of the various officials.										
3. Administrative organization should provide opportunity for the instructional staff to teach in their various departments without being overburdened with administrative duties.										
4. Administrative organization should provide, insofar as possible, for freeing the president from the performance of a multiplicity of duties which may occupy his time to such an extent that major attention cannot be given to the development of administrative and institutional policies.										
5. Administrative organization should provide for the utilization of an administrative council, chosen by the president to serve him in an advisory capacity concerning formation of policies and the making of administrative decisions, upon which the faculty as a whole is not informed. This criterion does not mean that final decision should be made by the council rather than the president.										
6. If an administrative council is used, the internal organization of the college should provide for faculty representation on the council.										
7. If an administrative council is used, it should consist of heads of departments.										
8. Administrative organization should provide special committees for investigations requiring special study.										
9. Administrative organization should provide for the selection of standing and special committees by the president.										
10. Administrative organization should provide for the selection of standing and special committees by the faculty or representatives of the faculty.										

A STATEMENT OF CRITERIA (*Continued*)

Please write (X) in the columns to the right opposite the word or words which best describe your judgment of the administrative condition represented by each criterion below. First, assume financial support reasonably adequate. Second, assume financial support curtailed or limited.	Financial Support Reasonably Adequate					Financial Support Curtailed or Limited				
	Highly Desirable	Desirable	Of No Particular Value But Not Undesirable	Undesirable	Harmful	Highly Desirable	Desirable	Of No Particular Value But Not Undesirable	Undesirable	Harmful
	1	2	3	4	5	1	2	3	4	5
11. Administrative organization should provide few, if any, standing committees for the administration of functions.										
12. Administrative organization should provide standing committees for the administration of all major groups of functions.										
13. Administrative organization should provide a fixed procedure for replacing membership in standing committees.										
14. When standing committees are used, administrative organization should provide for keeping membership and chairmanship constant insofar as possible.										
15. Administrative organization should provide for the participation of the whole faculty in suggesting or formulating policies concerning instruction.										
16. Administrative organization should provide for faculty approval of all major administrative policies.										
17. Administrative organization should provide for the grouping of related functions under the direction or control of an officer who in turn is responsible to the president.										
18. Administrative organization should provide for the centering of responsibility in individuals rather than in groups.										
19. Administrative organization should provide for the approval of policies by the state board of control.										
20. Administrative organization should provide for the making of final decisions by the president after policies have been approved by the state board of control. This criterion is not to be interpreted as interfering with the president's delegating to a subordinate officer authority to make decisions.										

APPENDIX B

THE INDEX RATING

In order to arrive at a value which would summarize the ratings given each criterion in Table II, page 11, the following procedure was used.

1. The terms used to characterize each criterion were assigned the following numerical values:

A.	Highly desirable	+ 1.0
B.	Desirable	+ 0.5
C.	Of no particular value but not undesirable	0.0
D.	Undesirable	− 0.5
E.	Harmful	− 1.0

2. Positive and negative values were assigned in order to have positive values indicate which criteria accompany sound administration and to have negative values indicate which criteria do not accompany sound administration.

3. The frequency with which each criterion was rated with one of the above characteristics was tabulated. The index rating was determined by multiplying each total frequency by the respective value assigned to the characteristics. These products were totaled and the sum was divided by the number of jurors who made ratings. The quotient which resulted is the index value.

4. Criterion 11, Table II was rated as follows: highly desirable, 12; desirable, 6; of no particular value but not undesirable, 0; undesirable, 11; harmful, 1. With these data the index value for criterion 11 was found as follows:

$$
\begin{aligned}
12 \times (1.0) &= +12 \\
6 \times (0.5) &= +3 \\
0 \times (0.0) &= 0 \\
11 \times (-0.5) &= -5.5 \\
1 \times (-1.0) &= -1 \\
\text{Sum} &= +8.5 \\
\text{Index rating} &= +8.5 \div 30 = +.28
\end{aligned}
$$

5. Index rating values were designated by dividing the range of rating values in five equal parts and labeling each as follows:

A.	Highly desirable	+0.6 to + 1.0
B.	Desirable	+0.2 to + .59
C.	Probably desirable	0.0 to + .19
	Probably undesirable	0.0 to − .19
D.	Undesirable	−0.2 to − .59
E.	Harmful	−0.6 to − 1.0